CHRISTMAS FUN FACTS!

a **KNOWLEDGE NUGGETS BOOK** *by*
❄ **MARIANNE JENNINGS** ❄

Christmas Fun Facts! From Advent to Xmas, Interesting Trivia and Amazing Fun Facts about Festive Holiday Traditions from around the World
Part of 'The Amazing Occasions Series'
Copyright © 2023 Knowledge Nugget Books
Willard, Utah & Liverpool, England
For permissions contact: hello@knowledgenuggetbooks.com

Book design by Paul-Hawkins.com
Edited by Joe Levit
Fact-checked by Hank Musolf

Library of Congress Control Number: 2023922576
ISBN 979-8-9884402-4-6 (paperback)
ISBN 979-8-9884402-5-3 (ebook)

www.knowledgenuggetbooks.com

christmas fun facts!

From Advent to Xmas, Interesting Trivia and
Amazing Fun Facts about Festive Holiday Traditions
from around the World

The Amazing Occasions Series

marianne jennings

KNOWLEDGE
NUGGET BOOKS

festive contents

proceed with festive caution!

The author cannot be held liable for a sudden inclination to belt out 'Silent Night' at inopportune moments, spontaneous urges to drink cocoa by the gallon, or newfound obsessions with twinkling lights.

Diving into this book won't endow you with the skill to wrap gifts with elf-like precision, lead a choir in flawless carol harmonies, or glide on ice without a single slip.

While every effort has been made to capture the spirit and facts of Yuletide, the author offers no guarantees against readers electing to dance with animated snowmen, challenge Krampus to a duel, or embark on epic quests to find the real Santa's workshop.

Be warned: *The magic of Christmas is even more captivating, warm, and wondrous than any book can convey!*

also by marianne jennings

So You Think You Know Canada, Eh?

This collection of silly & interesting facts is about Canada, the kind people who live there, all things maple syrup, hockey & lacrosse, its unique history, the breathtaking nature, & words to help you speak Canadian.

Amazing Alaska!

From glaciers to grizzlies, this #1 Bestseller in Alaska Travel is sure to surprise and delight readers who love anything and everything about Alaska. Packed with over 700 fun and interesting fun facts that even most locals don't know.

Everything About Astronauts Vol. 1 & Vol. 2

Teens and adults who love astronauts, fun facts, and little-known stories will find themselves mesmerized with over 1,400 interesting facts and out-of-world stories.

Quirky Careers & Offbeat Occupations
of the Past, Present, and Future

Explore a world where careers go beyond the ordinary 9 to 5. Whether you're intrigued by history, curious about niche careers, or dream of futuristic roles this collection of over 240 unique careers will entertain, educate, and inspire.

a jolly gift just for you!

Ho, ho, ho! As a token of appreciation for joining our festive journey, I've whipped up a FREE companion quiz e-book, brimming with over 100 jolly questions and answers straight from these pages.

Get your FREE festive quiz e-book right here:
🔗 https://bit.ly/christmas-factbook-bonus

SCAN ME

Challenge your friends, and spread the joy!
Merry Quizzing and Happy Holidays!

how to read this jolly book

Think of this book as your personal **Christmas tree,** each topic a twinkling ornament, ready to be admired.

You don't need to start with the star and work your way down; simply pick the sparkle that beckons your holiday heart and plunge into its fun festive facts.

And when you're filled with the spirit of the season, there's a merry quiz nestled at the back, ready to put your newfound Noel knowledge to the test.

Peek behind the final page for the answers, wrapped up like the last gift on Christmas morning.

jingle all the way through these pages!

Greetings, festive friend! Ever wondered why we hang stockings, or who shared the first Christmas card? You've ventured to the right snow-covered corner of the bookshelf!

This book is brimming with yuletide tales, age-old traditions, and sparkling snippets of facts that have shaped our Christmases for centuries.

Snuggle up with a blanket, let the aroma of cinnamon and pine fill the air, and prepare to be enchanted. By the time you close this book, you'll have a wealth of Christmas knowledge that could rival Santa Claus himself!

Here's to discoveries as delightful as the first snowfall.

Enjoy!

- Marianne

1
the origins of christmas

Pagan Festivals and Winter Solstice

I n the frosty embrace of winter, long before twinkling lights adorned our homes and jolly carols filled the air, ancient civilizations found warmth in the midst of the chill. These age-old communities celebrated the winter solstice, that magical day when the night is at its longest and daylight begins its return, promising the rebirth of spring. From grand bonfires that mimicked the sun's warmth to feasts that bolstered communal spirit, these Pagan festivals—such as the Roman Saturnalia or the Nordic Yule—paved the way for future festivities in the heart of winter.

winter solstice

The term "solstice" is derived from the Latin words "sol" (sun) and "sistere" (to stand still). During this celestial event, the sun appears momentarily stationary in the sky.

In the northern hemisphere, the December solstice is the winter solstice, marked by the shortest day and longest night of the year. Conversely, for those in the southern hemisphere, this is their summer solstice, with the longest day and shortest night. This event signifies the sun reaching its southernmost point in the sky. Days begin to lengthen in the north and shorten in the south post-solstice. Cultures around the world, both past and present, celebrate this significant solar occasion.

modern-day connection 🌑

The theme of light prevailing over darkness, commonly associated with the winter solstice, is also a theme in many Christian traditions related to the birth of Jesus.

stonehenge secrets 🪨

Sunset at Stonehenge. Photo by Iva Vanurova via depositphotos.com

During the winter solstice at Stonehenge, the sun creates a magical scene as it sets between two significant structures: the central Altar stone and the Slaughter stone. These structures form the largest trilithon, which consists of two upright stones supporting a horizontal stone on top. Today, Stonehenge draws thousands during both the winter and summer solstices. Attendees celebrate with song, dance, and festive attire, ensuring these ancient traditions continue to thrive.

candles & bonfires 🕯️

Candles and bonfires were a significant part of solstice celebrations. Lighting a fire was symbolic of the sun's return, driving away dark spirits and inviting warmth back to the land.

saturnalia 🎉

Saturnalia was an ancient Roman festival held in honor of the god Saturn. It was one of the most popular and long-standing festivals in Roman history, and laid the cultural groundwork for many modern Christmas traditions.

While Saturnalia was primarily a Pagan festival, many of its traditions—and the spirit of merrymaking, feasting, and gift-giving—carried forward into the celebrations of Christmas, especially after Christianity became the dominant religion of the Roman Empire.

saturnalia dates 📅

Saturnalia initially started on December 17, but eventually was expanded to a week-long festivity, lasting until December 23.

role reversals

One of the most distinct aspects of Saturnalia was the temporary reversal of societal roles. Masters served meals to their slaves, and the usual order of society was turned on its head. This was done to reflect the god Saturn's golden age, where peace and harmony prevailed.

feasting & gift giving

Much like Christmas today, Saturnalia was a time for feasting, and an exchange of gifts. Common gifts included small figurines, candles (symbolizing the increase of light after the solstice), and sigillaria (decorative earthenware).

holiday greetings

People would greet each other with a cheerful "Io Saturnalia!" (pronounced "yo"), which became a common exclamation throughout the holiday. "Io Saturnalia!" can be translated as "Hail Saturnalia!" or "Joyful Saturnalia!"

sol invictus celebration

The Romans had a festival called "Dies Natalis Solis Invicti," which translates to "the birthday of the unconquered sun," celebrated on December 25th. This was to honor the sun god and celebrate the sun's rebirth.

yule

Yule, or Yuletide, traces back to the midwinter festivities of the Germanic peoples, celebrating the promise of sunnier days ahead with feasts and joy. As Christianity found its way through Europe, some Yule customs, like the Yule log and the use of evergreens, became entwined with Christmas traditions. It's true the Norse celebrated Yule over several days during the winter solstice, but drawing a direct line to the Christian "Twelve Days of Christmas" might be an oversimplification, given their separate roots and symbolism.

yule log 🔥

The Yule log tradition, now practiced worldwide, has its origins in the customs of ancient Germanic peoples, including those from Nordic regions. Families would select a large log, bring it home with great ceremony, and burn it on the hearth. The burning symbolized the returning sun and served to ward off evil spirits. Today, many continue the practice of burning a Yule log during Christmas, while others enjoy a Yule log cake, a cherished dessert.

yule feasts 🍗

Yule was a significant feasting period for the Norse. As winter approached, they would slaughter animals they couldn't sustain throughout the colder months, leading to an abundance of fresh meat. While many culinary traditions have influenced today's Christmas feasts, they certainly echo the lavishness of those ancient Yule celebrations.

The Germanic and Norse people were distinct groups in ancient Northern Europe. The Germanic folks came from different parts of Europe, spoke various Germanic languages, and had their own gods and myths. Meanwhile, the Norse people were from Scandinavia, spoke Old Norse, and had special gods like Odin, Thor, and Loki. Even though they lived close to each other, they were not exactly the same. The Norse were like a smaller group within the larger Germanic family.

Over time, some of their beliefs and traditions, like celebrating the winter solstice with Yule, mixed together and evolved into what we now know as Christmas traditions. So, while they had their differences, they also influenced the holiday we celebrate today!

— Did Yule Know?!

---

yule goat 🐐

The Yule Goat, a festive symbol with roots in Scandinavia and Northern Europe, originates from ancient Pagan traditions associated with the Norse god Thor, who had two goats pulling his chariot.

Over time, as Christianity spread, the Yule Goat's Pagan significance blended into Christian celebrations. In modern traditions, its representation varies. For instance, in Sweden, a large straw Yule Goat is erected in the town of Gävle annually, while in Finland, the once mischievous "Joulupukki" or "Christmas Goat" has evolved into a Santa Claus-like figure, gifting presents to children.

father christmas origins 🎅

The "Jultomten" or "Julenisse" is a gnome-like creature from Scandinavian folklore, who brought gifts during Yule. This figure has evolved over time, blending with other European gift-bringers, to contribute to the modern image of Father Christmas or Santa Claus.

wassailing 🍷

Wassailing has its roots in Anglo-Saxon traditions, where participants would toast to good health and a bountiful harvest. The word 'wassail' comes from the Old English salutation 'wes þu hāl', which means 'be in good health'. Over time, the custom evolved, and today, wassailing often refers to the festive act of singing carols from house to house during the Christmas season.

twelve days 🥁

The Norse observed Yule, a midwinter festival that spanned several days around the winter solstice, which some believe may have lasted up to 12 days. Separately, in Christian traditions, the "Twelve Days of Christmas" span from Christmas Day to Epiphany on January 6th

mistletoe 💋

In Norse mythology, Balder, a beloved god, met his end by a weapon fashioned from mistletoe, orchestrated by the trickster Loki. In the aftermath, it's said that Balder's mother, Frigg, shed tears that became the plant's white berries. She then declared mistletoe a symbol of love and peace. While this tale is a testament to the plant's significance in Norse lore, the tradition of kissing under the mistletoe also draws from broader European customs that revered the plant for its fertility and life-affirming properties.

yule boar

Before the Yule goat became popular, there was the Yule boar. Families would pledge oaths on the boar's bristles during feasts. Today, while the boar symbolism is less common, dishes like the Swedish "julskinka" (Christmas ham) can trace their roots back to this tradition.

continuous light

During the Yule season, given the extended darkness of northern winters, it was common for people to keep candles burning and fires lit. This practice not only provided essential warmth and light but also symbolized hope and resilience against the cold dark days. While the direct lineage to modern Christmas lights isn't exact, the human instinct to seek and celebrate light during the darkest times of the year remains a shared sentiment, manifesting today in our bright and festive holiday decorations.

evergreen décor

In ancient times, including among the Norse, evergreens were cherished symbols of resilience during the bleak winter months. Their enduring greenery offered a beacon of hope, hinting at life's continuation amid the cold. These early cultures often brought evergreen branches into their homes, a practice that echoed the promise of an impending spring.

While the precise origins of the modern Christmas tree are debated, this tradition of honoring evergreens undeniably influenced our contemporary holiday customs. Today, our festive Christmas trees and wreaths can be traced back to these ancient gestures of hope and celebration.

deck the halls

The popular Christmas carol, 'Deck the Halls,' features the line about 'trolling the ancient Yuletide carol,' which means to sing a festive song with gusto. While the melody hails from an old Welsh winter tune and mentions 'Yuletide,' a term associated with ancient winter celebrations, the modern lyrics don't directly reference Pagan Yule practices.

2
the birth of jesus

History vs. Tradition

S tep into the magical world of Christmas where history and tradition collide! Ever wondered about the guiding star of the Magi or where the "X" in Xmas comes from? So, gather 'round the manger, and let's dive into the delightful debate of The Birth of Jesus: History vs Tradition!

star-lit guide ⭐

While the Bible mentions the appearance of a star that guided the Magi to Jesus, it doesn't specify its nature. Some speculate it might have been a comet, a supernova, or even a rare conjunction of planets. Talk about a celestial event!

room for debate 🏠

The traditional image is that Jesus was born in a stable because there was "no room at the inn." However, some scholars believe "inn" might be better translated as "guest room," and suggest

Jesus might have been born in the main living area of a crowded house instead of a separate stable.

gift-bearing visitors 👳

We commonly refer to the Magi as "Three Kings" thanks to the song, but the Bible doesn't specify their number or that they were kings. The assumption of three comes from the three gifts they brought: gold, frankincense, and myrrh.

frankincense & myrrh? 🏺

The were not random. Frankincense, a fragrant resin, was often used in worship, hinting at the divine. Myrrh, also a resin, was used for anointing and burial, foreshadowing Jesus' future.

manger scene mix-up 🐑

Nativity scenes often show sheep, oxen, and even camels around baby Jesus. However, the Bible doesn't mention any animals present at his birth. These additions might come from non-biblical texts or simply make the scene more picturesque.

angelic announcements 👼

Angels played the role of divine messengers for the birth of Jesus. While we often see a single angel in nativity stories telling the shepherds about the birth, the Bible mentions "a great company of the heavenly host." That's basically an angelic flash mob!

mary's mode of transport 🐴

Many depict Mary traveling to Bethlehem on a donkey, especially in children's stories. However, the Bible doesn't specify how she got there. She could've walked or used another mode of transportation. The donkey just adds a touch of rustic charm!

date dilemmas & the december 25th mystery 📅

Despite Christmas being celebrated on December 25th, the Bible doesn't provide an exact birth date for Jesus. Early Christians chose this date because it coincided with Pagan festivals, turning the focus to the birth of Christ.

The reason for choosing December 25th remains debated. One theory is that it was selected to coincide with the Roman festival of Saturnalia and the winter solstice, making it easier to convert Pagans to Christianity by "Christianizing" popular Pagan celebrations.

christmas... in the summer? ☀

Some researchers, based on clues about shepherds and their flocks in the Bible, speculate that Jesus might have been born in the spring or summer. However, the exact timing remains one of history's intriguing puzzles.

from cristes maesse to christmas 🕊

The word "Christmas" has its origins in the Old English phrase "Cristes maesse," which means "Christ's mass." "Cristes" refers to Christ, and "maesse" is an old word for "mass" or religious service.

The earliest recorded use of the word "Christmas" dates back to the 11th century in Old English writings, although the celebration of Christ's birth predates this term.

Over time, "Cristes maesse" evolved into "Cristemasse" in Middle English. This later transformed into "Christemmas" before finally becoming "Christmas."

christmas in different languages

While "Christmas" is the common term used in English-speaking countries, the holiday is known by different names in other languages. For example, in Spanish, it's "Navidad," in French, it's "Noël," in Portuguese, it's "Natal," and in Swedish, Norwegian and Danish, it's "Jul."

diverse dates of christmas

Not all Christians celebrate Christmas on December 25. In some countries, such as Russia and Greece, Christmas Day falls on January 7th.

Christmas falls on January 7th in Russia and Greece because these countries follow the Julian calendar for religious observances. While most of the world switched to the Gregorian calendar, which celebrates Christmas on December 25th, the Eastern Orthodox Church, including Russia and Greece, retained the Julian calendar, causing a 13-day difference in the date of Christmas celebrations.

why 'x' in xmas?

The abbreviation "Xmas" for "Christmas" originates from the Greek letter "Chi", which looks like an "X" and is the first letter of the Greek word for "Christ." Early Christians used "X" as a shorthand for "Christ", and over time, this merged with "mas", a shortened form of the Old English word for the Christian celebration. Despite its religious origins, some today view "Xmas" as secular or disrespectful, though its roots are deeply Christian.

3
the christmas tree

Huddle close, dear reader, and let's venture on a jolly journey through the twinkling world of Christmas trees! From their fragrant evergreen branches to the cherished ornaments they bear, these festive firs have spruced up our holidays for centuries. But, oh! The stories they could tell if they could only talk.

Ready to unwrap the secrets of the world's most famous pines? On Dasher, on Dancer, let's dive into a forest of fun facts!

fir-tastic origins 🎄

Did you know the evergreen fir tree has traditionally been used to celebrate winter festivals—both Pagan and Christian—for thousands of years? The green branches serve as a vivid reminder that spring will return.

german beginnings 🇩🇪

O Tannenbaum! The literal translation of the word "tannenbaum" means fir tree in German. The tradition of the indoor Christmas tree started in Germany in the 16th century. Instead of the lovely ornaments we have today, they used fruits like apples, nuts, and paper flowers to decorate their trees.

global growth 🌍

From Germany, the Christmas tree trend spread across the world. In fact, there are approximately 25-30 million real Christmas trees sold in the United States every year.

lighting the way 💡

In 1882, the first electrically lit Christmas tree was introduced by Thomas Edison's friend and associate, Edward H. Johnson. He decorated a Christmas tree with a string of 80 red, white, and blue electric light bulbs in his New York City home. Before then, trees were illuminated with candles. Talk about a fire hazard!

ornament origins 🍎

One of the first Christmas tree ornaments were apples, meant to represent the Tree of Knowledge from the Christian tradition. As the practice continued, people began to replace the apples with other decorations—first paper flowers and Communion wafers, and eventually more varied and intricate ornaments. This evolved into the rich tradition of decorating Christmas trees with diverse ornaments that we see nowadays. Today, there's no limit to the creativity of tree decorations!

topper tales ✨

The star or angel atop the Christmas tree represents the Star of Bethlehem or the angel that announced Jesus's birth. However, nowadays, from ribbons to family heirlooms, anything can become a tree topper!

royal approval 👑

Christmas Tree at Windsor Castle, drawn by J. L. Williams. Illustration for The Illustrated London News, Christmas Number 1848. Joseph Lionel Williams, Public domain, via Wikimedia Commons

Britain caught onto the Christmas tree trend when Queen Victoria's German husband, Prince Albert, set up a tree in Windsor Castle in 1841. Prince Albert grew up in Germany, where the Christmas tree, or "Weihnachtsbaum," was already an established tradition. It was customary for German families to decorate these trees with candles, sweets, and small toys.

A few years later, in 1848, an illustration was published in the "Illustrated London News" depicting Queen Victoria, Prince Albert, and their children around a Christmas tree. This image had a significant impact on the British public. If the Christmas tree was good enough for the monarchy, it was good enough for the masses! The practice quickly gained popularity among the British elite and middle class.

Given the influence of the British Empire during the 19th century, this trend wasn't confined to just Britain. The royal Christmas tree was emulated in homes across the empire, influencing traditions in countries far beyond the British Isles.

a gifted base 🎁

Placing gifts under the tree dates back to when it was believed Santa Claus would place them there while children slept. Now, it's a delightful tradition that many eagerly anticipate on Christmas morning.

christmas tree farmers 🪓

Christmas tree farmers work year-round to bring festive cheer to your homes. These dedicated growers nurture and tend to various tree varieties like Fraser or Balsam firs in their fields for several years before they become the centerpiece of your holiday celebrations.

Depending on the tree, it can take roughly 6-10 years for a tree to grow to a typical height of 6-7 feet or 1.8 to 2.1 meters.

Before she became a global pop sensation, Taylor Swift spent her childhood on a Pennsylvania Christmas tree farm. Her family owned and operated the farm, where they would cultivate Scotch pine and Fraser fir trees, and sell the trees to families during the holiday season.

Swift's experiences on the farm inspired her to write a song titled "Christmas Tree Farm," which she released in 2019.

— Did Yule Know?!

different countries prefer different christmas trees

When it comes to choosing the perfect Christmas tree, different countries have certain preferences. This depends on cultural traditions, personal preferences, and what's available.

United States: In the United States, the most popular Christmas tree species varies by region. In the Pacific Northwest, the Douglas fir is a favorite due to its iconic pyramid shape and sweet fragrance. In the Northeast, the Balsam fir and Fraser fir are popular choices, known for their sturdy branches and pleasant scents.

Canada: Canadians have eight different varieties to choose from when it comes to Christmas trees, including the Balsam Fir, Scots Pine, White Spruce, White Pine, Noble Fir, Fraser Fir, Colorado Blue Spruce, and Douglas Fir.

But according to Christmas Tree farms in Canada, the Scots Pine, also known as the Scotch Pine, is the most popular among Canadians. The Scots Pine is a tall, triangular, and vibrant green Christmas tree. It's known for being incredibly low-maintenance because it doesn't shed many needles, even as it dries out during the holiday season.

Germany: The Nordmann fir is highly favored in Germany. It has soft needles that are not prickly, making it a great choice for families with young children. Its symmetrical shape and excellent needle retention also contribute to its popularity.

United Kingdom: Nordmann fir and Norway spruce are both popular choices in the UK. Nordmann firs are known for their balanced shape and low needle drop, while Norway spruces have a more traditional look.

The Scandinavian Countries: Norway spruce is often chosen for Christmas trees in Scandinavian countries like Sweden and Denmark. It has a conventional look with dense branches and a classic Christmas tree scent.

Australia: In Australia, where Christmas falls during the summer months, some people opt for artificial trees, or choose native plants like the Norfolk Island pine as alternatives to traditional Christmas trees.

France: Blue spruce and Nordmann fir are popular choices for Christmas trees in France. Blue spruce is valued for its distinctive blue-green color and stiff branches that can support heavy decorations.

🇲🇽 🌵 🎄 **Parts of Mexico, Southwestern United States & the Caribbean:** In some places, traditional fir or pine trees aren't readily available, so local plants are used to showcase the festive spirit. In deserts, cacti are often decorated with lights and ornaments. Places that are more tropical will decorate palm trees.

famous trees around the world

Famous Norway spruce outside the Rockefeller Center in NYC. Photo by Kaydn Ito on Unsplash

The Rockefeller Center Tree 🇺🇸
Location: New York City, USA
Fun Fact: One of the most iconic Christmas trees in the

world, this Norway spruce annually stands between 65 to 100 feet (20 to 30 meters) tall. After the holiday season, the lumber from the tree is donated to Habitat for Humanity to be used in house construction.

Trafalgar Square Christmas Tree 🏴
Location: London, England
Fun Fact: This tree is an annual gift from Norway to the UK as a token of gratitude for Britain's support during World War II. The tradition dates back to 1947.

Sao Paulo's Ibirapuera Christmas Tree 🇧🇷
Location: Sao Paulo, Brazil
Fun Fact: This tree is often one of the tallest artificial Christmas trees in the world, illuminated with millions of LED lights.

Dortmund Christmas Tree 🇩🇪
Location: Dortmund, Germany
Fun Fact: Arguably the world's largest Christmas tree, this tree is actually made up of 1,700 individual fir trees and stands at an impressive 147 feet or 45 meters tall.

Vatican Christmas Tree 🇻🇦
Location: Vatican City
Fun Fact: Standing in Saint Peter's Square, this tree is illuminated by energy-saving lights, aligning with the Vatican's environmental concerns.

Boston's Gifted Tree from Nova Scotia 🇨🇦🇺🇸
Location: Boston, USA
Fun Fact: Every year, Nova Scotia sends a Christmas tree to Boston, a tradition born from gratitude and friendship dating back to 1917, following the Halifax Explosion, a devastating event in Canadian history. After the explosion, which was caused by a collision of two ships and resulted in extensive damage, deaths, and injuries, Boston swiftly sent aid to Halifax, deeply touching its people. In 1918, to express their thanks, Nova Scotia gifted Boston a Christmas tree, a gesture that evolved into an annual tradition starting in 1971.

Manger Square Christmas Tree 🇵🇸
Location: Bethlehem, Palestine
Fun Fact: Manger Square is in the center of Bethlehem and gets its name from the manger where Christ is said to have been born. The massive Christmas Tree and the lighting ceremony is highly symbolic and the decorations are often a blend of local Palestinian culture with Christian traditions. Since 2011, the Christmas Decorators of Liverpool, England with the help of Palestinian volunteers, have been responsible for decorating this special tree in this extra special place.

the first christmas tree lights 💡

The invention of Christmas lights is credited to Thomas Edison, the renowned American inventor. In the late 19th century, Edison's invention of practical incandescent light bulbs paved the way for the creation of Christmas lights.

In 1880, Edison's friend and associate, Edward H. Johnson, became the first to decorate a Christmas tree with electric lights. He hand-wired 80 red, white, and blue bulbs, and showcased the illuminated tree in his New York City home. This early display of electric Christmas lights by Johnson marked the beginning of a new era in festive decorations.

The first commercially available Christmas lights were introduced in 1890 by the Edison General Electric Company. They were expensive, and only the wealthiest individuals could afford them.

star struck

The star atop Christmas trees represents the Star of Bethlehem, which is believed to have guided the three kings, or magi, to the newborn Jesus. It signifies divine guidance and hope.

4
iconic christmas symbols

Unwrap the stories behind beloved Christmas symbols like mistletoe, candy canes, and festive bells. Discover the historical roots and cultural variations of these cherished symbols as we delve into the heartwarming traditions that have come to define the holiday season.

merry mistletoe! 🌿

The belief in mistletoe's magical properties can be traced back to the Druids, and ancient Norse mythology. The Druids thought that this winter-blooming plant could ward off evil spirits and bring good luck. Kissing under the mistletoe became popular in Victorian England, symbolizing love and friendship.

angelic announcements 👼

Angels are integral to the Christmas story. According to the Bible, they announced Jesus' birth— first to Mary, then to

Joseph, and finally to the shepherds. These angels symbolize heavenly joy and the message of hope and salvation.

the nativity 🐄

The nativity scene, also known as a crèche, originated with St. Francis of Assisi in the 13th century. He wanted to emphasize the importance of the birth of Jesus and created the first live nativity scene in Greccio, Italy, using animals and people to recreate the scene.

According to legend, St. Francis included an ox and a donkey in the first nativity scene, even though they are not mentioned in the biblical account. The ox symbolized patience, and the donkey represented humility.

nativity scenes around the world

The nativity scene is not exclusive to Christianity's Western traditions. It has been adopted by cultures worldwide, each adding its own cultural flair. For example, in Mexico, nativity scenes often include tasks from daily life, such as people making tortillas.

candy canes 🍬

Candy canes, with their historical origins dating back to 17th-century Europe, have become an iconic symbol of Christmas. Their symbolic shape represents the shepherd's crook or the letter "J" for Jesus, with white denoting purity and red symbolizing Christ's sacrifice.

Legend has it that candy canes were created in 1670 by a German choirmaster to keep the choirboys quiet during long nativity services. Pulled sweets were all the rage at the time, but they came in the form of straight sticks. To be appropriate to have in church, the theory is that a hook was added to resemble a shepherd's crook.

In modern Christmas traditions, candy canes adorn trees, serve as stocking stuffers, and feature in various crafts.

christmas stockings 🧦

Christmas stockings have a fascinating history, with legends dating back to ancient Turkey. Today, the tradition of hanging stockings is widespread. It typically involves placing empty stockings near the fireplace or at the foot of the bed on Christmas Eve and children eagerly await the surprises Santa leaves behind. These stockings come in various sizes, and small gifts, known as "stocking stuffers," are placed inside.

In some countries, children leave out shoes or boots instead of stockings for Santa to fill. In France, it's Père Noël who fills children's shoes, while in the Netherlands, it's Sinterklaas who leaves gifts in wooden shoes called "klompen."

advent 🕯️

Advent is a Christian tradition that occurs during the four weeks leading up to Christmas. The word "Advent" comes from the Latin word "adventus," which means "coming" or "arrival."

Advent focuses on preparing for the celebration of Jesus Christ's birth. Each week has a specific theme represented by the lighting of candles on an Advent wreath: hope, peace, joy, and love. Some Advent wreaths also include a central fifth candle, known as the "Christ Candle." This candle is typically lit on Christmas Eve or Christmas Day and represents the arrival of Christ.

Advent involves reading relevant Scripture passages, attending church services, and performing acts of kindness. It's a time for reflection and joyful anticipation of Christmas, observed by various Christian denominations.

advent calendars 📅

The tradition of advent calendars dates back to the 19th century in Germany. Early versions involved counting down the days to Christmas using chalk marks on doors or candles.

The first printed advent calendar is credited to Gerhard Lang in the early 20th century. He created a calendar with 24 little doors to open, each revealing a Christmas image.

The concept of advent calendars with small chocolates behind the doors became popular in the mid-20th century. These edible surprises added an extra layer of excitement for kids and adults alike.

The tradition of advent calendars has spread around the world and is not limited to Christian communities. People of various backgrounds enjoy the anticipation and joy of counting down to the holiday season.

christingles 🍊

A Christingle is a symbolic object used in Christian Advent and Christmas celebrations, consisting of an orange representing the world, a red ribbon around it symbolizing Christ's love and blood, dried fruits and sweets skewered on four sticks pushed into the orange, indicating the four seasons and God's creations; and a candle inserted into the top of the orange, signifying Jesus Christ as the light of the world.

This charming tradition originated in the Moravian Church in Germany in 1747 as a simple method to convey the message of Jesus to children. Today, Christingles have evolved into a globally embraced custom, often linked with charity efforts, particularly for children's causes.

festive feathers

Doves have long held a revered place in the tapestry of Christmas. These elegant birds, symbols of peace and purity, are deeply intertwined with the narrative of the festive season. As in the biblical tale of the ark, where the dove announced hope by presenting an olive branch, doves have consistently signaled new beginnings and divine reassurances. Come Christmastime, the dove takes flight in songs, stories, and decorations, embodying the timeless message of peace on Earth. When a dove graces a Christmas setting, it does more than just adorn; it whispers of serenity and the profound hope the season promises.

the jolly jingle

Bells have resonated with the spirit of Christmas for centuries. Their tones, both solemn and celebratory, have historically announced significant events, from the birth of the Savior to communal gatherings. They've found their way into timeless carols, been hung as festive decorations, and symbolized moments of unity and reflection during the season. The familiar chime of the Salvation Army bell ringers stands as a testament to this, serving as both a reminder of the season and a call to compassion. So, when a bell tolls this Christmas, it carries with it the weight and tradition of many Christmases past.

ho-ho-holly!

Holly's prickly leaves are thought to represent the crown of thorns that Jesus wore, with the red berries symbolizing the drops of blood he shed. Romans gifted holly wreaths during Saturnalia, and early Christians adopted it, reinterpreting its meaning.

poinsettia power

Poinsettia plant. Photo by Jeffrey Hamilton on Unsplash

This bright red plant is native to Mexico and was named after Joel Roberts Poinsett, the first U.S. Ambassador to Mexico, who introduced it to America in the 1820s. A popular Mexican legend tells the tale of a poor girl named Pepita who, unable to afford a gift for the baby Jesus on Christmas Eve, was inspired by an angel to pick weeds from the roadside and place them in front of the church altar. Miraculously, they bloomed into bright red poinsettias.

While red poinsettias are the most popular, they also come in white, pink, and even marbled varieties. The poinsettia's vibrant leaves are thought to symbolize the Star of Bethlehem, which led the Wise Men to Jesus. The red color represents the blood of Christ, making it a fitting decoration for Christmas celebrations.

Poinsettias have been associated with Christmas for over 400 years, making them one of the holiday's oldest floral traditions.

Poinsettias Have Red Leaves, Not Red Flowers

What many consider the "flowers" of the poinsettia are actually specialized leaves called bracts. The true flowers are the small, yellow buds located in the center of the bracts.

Poinsettias are considered to be mildly toxic to dogs and cats and can cause them to have an upset stomach. So best to keep the poinsettias away from our furry friends.

— Did Yule Know?!

---

christmas crackers

A Christmas cracker. Photo by Stuartbur via depositphotos.com

A Christmas cracker is a festive holiday tradition originating in the UK but now popular in many parts of the world. It's a colorful, paper-wrapped tube meant to be pulled apart by two people, creating a loud "crack." Inside, you'll find a paper crown to wear, a small gift or toy, and a festive joke or riddle. Placed at each table setting during Christmas dinner, pulling crackers adds a whimsical and surprising element to the celebration.

Christmas crackers have been a tradition for over 170 years. They were first created in the early 1840s by a British confectioner named Tom Smith. Initially, they were simple sweets wrapped in decorative paper.

Inside the cracker, you'll also find a slip of paper with a festive joke or riddle. These jokes are often groan-worthy puns or play on words, and they are meant for everyone to understand and to add humor to the occasion.

gingerbread goodness

Gingerbread and Christmas have a deliciously intertwined history. Originating from medieval Europe, gingerbread's rich spices were said to have medicinal properties, which made it a favored treat for special occasions. By the time of the holidays, intricately designed gingerbread cookies and houses became a festive tradition. Their warm spices like ginger and cinnamon evoke the cozy feel of the season. Today, creating gingerbread houses and cookies remains a delightful Christmas activity, bringing together family and friends to celebrate and savor the flavors of the holidays.

coal in your stocking

The quirky tradition of leaving coal for naughty kids at Christmas is like a playful nudge from Santa: "Be good or else!" Long ago, coal, a common yet not-so-exciting item, was chosen as the perfect 'anti-gift' for those on the naughty list. It's all about encouraging good behavior, with coal standing in funny contrast to the cool presents good kids receive. Nowadays, this old-school tradition gets a twist, with 'coal' often being yummy chocolate treats disguised as lumps of coal.

christmas cards

The concept of sending holiday greetings dates back to ancient civilizations, where people exchanged tokens of goodwill to celebrate the winter solstice. Early Christians also exchanged handwritten messages to convey blessings during the festive season.

The first commercially produced Christmas card was also the

A variety of Christmas cards. Photo by Annie Spratt on Unsplash

first mass-produced Christmas card printed and sold in the United Kingdom. It was designed by Sir Henry Cole in 1843. The card was a lithograph that depicted a Christmas dinner with three generations of a family enjoying a party with side panels showed charitable scenes of people clothing and feeding the poor. It read "A Merry Christmas and a Happy New Year to You." Only 12 of the original 1,000 cards still exist.

The first mass-produced Christmas card printed and sold in the UK. Public Domain photo via WikiCommons.

The most expensive Christmas card was one of the first commercially produced Christmas cards. It was one of only a dozen of the original 1,000 known to have survived to the present day. In 2001, one of these rare gems, sent by Sir Arthur Cole to his mother, commanded a staggering £20,000 ($28,000) at auction, securing its place as the most valuable Christmas card ever sold.

— Did Yule Know?

The first Christmas card in the United States was printed in 1875 by Louis Prang & Company. Prang was a German immigrant who had a successful business printing greeting cards.

The first Christmas card to feature Santa Claus was printed in 1885 by Thomas Nast. Nast was an American cartoonist who is best known for his illustrations of Santa Claus.

Different cultures and countries have their own unique traditions associated with Christmas and holiday cards. In Japan, sending New Year's cards, known as "nengajo," is a common practice. In Spain, 'El Gordo,' a special Christmas lottery, is widely publicized, and people often send lottery tickets as holiday greetings.

In the UK, the tradition of sending Christmas cards began in the Victorian era and remains popular today, with many featuring iconic British symbols like robins and the Royal family.

Meanwhile, in Australia, Christmas cards often reflect the summer season, showcasing beaches, barbecues, and native wildlife. Each nation brings its own flavor to the season's greetings, reflecting its cultural nuances and traditions.

According to a survey by the Greeting Card Association, snowmen are the most popular Christmas card design, followed by Santa Claus, reindeer, and angels.

According to the same survey, red is the most popular Christmas card color, followed by green, gold, and silver.

The survey also claims "Merry Christmas" is the most popular Christmas card sentiment, followed by "Happy Holidays" and "Season's Greetings."

— Did Yule Know?!

---

christmas updates & newsletters

Sending Christmas letters with family updates is a relatively recent, but widespread tradition where people share highlights, news, and personal updates with friends and distant relatives via Christmas cards. These letters typically feature anecdotes, achievements, and photos in a festive tone, fostering connections during the holiday season.

5

from st. nicholas to father christmas

The Many Faces of Santa

F rom the humble origins of **Saint Nicholas** to the global phenomenon of Santa Claus, this chapter unveils the fascinating evolution of the beloved gift-bringer. Explore traditions like Christmas stockings and discover the diverse names and outfits Santa dons across the world.

santa claus & st. nicholas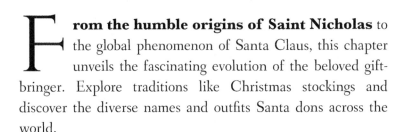

The modern-day Santa Claus is based on the figure of Saint Nicholas a 4th-century bishop from Myra (modern-day Turkey). Known for his generosity and kindness, Saint Nicholas would secretly gift coins to those in need. The Dutch brought the story of Saint Nicholas to America, where he eventually evolved into the Santa Claus we know and love today.

st. nicholas & christmas stockings

The tradition of hanging stockings is said to have originated from a story about St. Nicholas. He helped a poor man by secretly dropping a bag of gold down his chimney, which landed in a stocking that was hanging by the fire to dry. This act of kindness led to the custom of children hanging stockings by the fireplace or at the foot of their bed in hopes of receiving gifts from St. Nicholas or Santa Claus. Over time, the tradition has evolved into a cherished part of Christmas celebrations around the world.

the different names of santa

Depending on where you are, Santa has different names! Here are a few you may or may not know:

 Santa Claus (USA & Canada)

In the USA and Canada, Santa Claus is the most common name used. The name "Santa Claus" evolved from the Dutch "Sinterklaas," which refers to St. Nicholas.

The modern image of Santa Claus, with his red suit and white beard, was created in Thomas Nast who first drew an illustration of Santa in 1862 for the Christmas edition of New York's *Harper's Weekly* magazine cover and was popularized by Coca-Cola advertisements in the 1930s.

The first illustration of Santa created by Thomas Nast.
Public domain, via Wikimedia Commons

🇬🇧 Father Christmas (UK)

In the UK, "Father Christmas" has ancient roots and was asso-ciated with medieval celebrations of Christmas. He tradition-ally wore a green or brown robe, reflecting the English countryside.

🇫🇷 Père Noël (France)

In France, "Père Noël" means "Father Christmas." The term became widely used in the 19th century and is the figure who brings gifts to children on Christmas Eve.

🇨🇦 Santa Claus & Père Noël (Canada)

In Canada, the holiday spirit embraces a bilingual twist! While many know the jolly old fellow who delivers gifts to children as Santa Claus, in the French-speaking regions of the country, he's also affectionately called "Père Noël". This dual naming reflects Canada's rich bilingual heritage, with English and French being the two official languages.

🇩🇪 Weihnachtsmann (Germany)

The "Weihnachtsmann" is the Christmas gift-bringer in Germany. He is often depicted as wearing a long robe and carrying a sack of gifts, similar to the American Santa Claus.

🇳🇱 Sinterklaas (Netherlands)

Sinterklaas. Photo by twixx via depositphotos.com

Sinterklaas or Sint-Nicolaas is a Dutch figure based on St. Nicholas and is celebrated on the evening of St. Nicholas' Eve or December 5th. He arrives from Spain traditionally on a white horse and is accompanied by his helper, Zwarte Piet, and delivers gifts to well-behaved children.

San Nicolás (Venezuela)
In Venezuela, "San Nicolás" is associated with the Feast of St. Nicholas on December 6th, a tradition reflecting the country's European cultural influences. He is portrayed as a bishop and brings gifts to children on this day.

Ded Moroz (Russia)
"Ded Moroz," meaning "Grandfather Frost," is the Russian counterpart to Santa Claus. He is often depicted as a bearded figure wearing a long coat and a staff.

Joulupukki (Finland)
"Joulupukki," which translates to "Yule Goat," is the Finnish Santa figure. Originally, Joulupukki was a malevolent spirit, but over time, he transformed into a benevolent gift-giver.

Hoteiosho (Japan)
In Japan, "Hoteiosho" is a bearded Buddhist monk who bears gifts to children on New Year's Eve. The gift-giving tradition aligns with the Japanese New Year celebrations.

Viejito Pascuero (Chile)
"Viejito Pascuero," is a name affectionately used in Chile for Santa and translates to "Old Man Christmas." He can be found delivering gifts via front doors or windows (as chimneys aren't as common in Chile and sometimes arriving on horseback or by boat.

 Kersvader (South Africa)

In South Africa, "Kersvader" directly translates to "Christmas Father" in Afrikaans. Christmas falls during the summertime in South Africa and while Kersvader is often depicted as a jolly man in a red suit and white beard, he often dons an outfit that suits the local climate.

▮▮ Babbo Natale (Italy)

"Babbo Natale" translates to "Father Christmas" in Italian. He is often depicted as wearing a red suit and brings gifts to children on Christmas Eve.

leaving food for santa

The tradition of children leaving treats for Santa Claus varies across different cultures and countries, adding unique touches to this charming custom.

🇺🇸 🇨🇦 United States and Canada

Children in the U.S. and Canada often leave a glass of milk and cookies for Santa and often a carrot or two for Santa's reindeer.

🇬🇧🇮🇪 UK and Ireland

Children in the UK and Ireland often leave out mince pies and a glass of sherry or a non-alcoholic drink for Father Christmas.

🇦🇺 Australia

Due to the Southern Hemisphere's hot weather during Christmas, Australians sometimes leave out cold drinks or beer for Santa, along with treats.

 Netherlands

In the Netherlands, children may leave out shoes, sometimes filled with hay or carrots for Santa's reindeer, along with a treat for Sinterklaas (St. Nicholas).

Sweden

Children in Sweden might leave out a bowl of porridge for the "Yule Goat" or "Julbock," which is a Christmas figure in Scandinavian folklore.

Germany

In some regions of Germany, children leave out a plate of biscuits or treats for the "Christkind" or "Weihnachtsmann."

France

In France, children might leave out a shoe or a stocking for Père Noël along with treats.

international wardrobe

Step into Santa's global closet and discover the festive fashion from around the world! From traditional robes to unique twists, each Santa outfit reflects the spirit of the season and the diversity of cultures. Join us on a merry journey through Santa's international wardrobe!

🇺🇸 🇨🇦 United States & Canada

The iconic red and white suit of the American and Canadian Santa Claus is often credited to Coca-Cola's advertisements in the 1930s. However, it was influenced by earlier depictions of Santa in a red suit from various sources, including the Thomas Nast illustration in the New York magazine, *Harper's Weekly* in 1862.

🇬🇧 United Kingdom

Father Christmas in the UK most often wears red, but sometimes dons a green robe, inspired by medieval depictions. This attire reflects the lush countryside and evergreen landscapes, creating a distinct look.

🇫🇷 France

Père Noël wears a long red cloak with white fur trim, similar to the American Santa. He might also sport a blue hooded robe, known as a "capuchon."

🇩🇪 Germany

The German Weihnachtsmann wears a long red coat with white fur trim and often carries a sack of gifts. He may also sport a bishop-like mitre or hood, a nod to the influence of St. Nicholas.

🇮🇹 Italy

Babbo Natale in Italy wears a red suit with white fur trim, similar to the American Santa. He might also wear a hat with a tassel or pom-pom.

🇳🇱 Netherlands

Sinterklaas wears a bishop's robe, mitre, and carries a staff. His traditional attire dates back to the historical figure of St. Nicholas, upon whom the character is based.

🇷🇺 Russia

Ded Moroz, the Russian gift-bringer, often wears a long blue or red robe with white fur trim, along with a long white beard. His appearance has evolved over time.

🇫🇮 Finland

Joulupukki, originally a feared "Yule Goat" in Finnish tradition, demanding gifts and scaring children, has evolved into a benevolent Christmas figure similar to Santa Claus. He is now portrayed wearing a red or green robe with a fur-trimmed hat.

🇦🇺 Australia

Australian Santa in shorts. Photo rendered by
MidJourney by the author.

In Australia, where Christmas falls during summer, Santa might be depicted wearing a red suit with shorts and sunglasses, reflecting the warm climate.

Japan

Hoteiosho, the Japanese gift-giver, is sometimes depicted as a Buddhist monk with a red robe and sack of presents, blending traditional attire with the holiday theme.

a very santa occupation

Did you know in the United States, there are schools specifically for Santa's? Aspiring St. Nicks attend these schools to master the art of "Ho-ho-ho!-ing," perfect their jolly appearance, and learn the intricacies of reindeer care.

letters to santa

Every Christmas, Santa Claus receives around one million letters from around the world, some as far away as New Zealand or South Africa.

Santa Claus has a few different addresses you can send your letters to. It doesn't matter which address you send your letter to Santa, but some of his special mailing addresses may be closer to you than others.

Here are a just few to choose from:

If you're in Canada, send your letters to:

> Santa Claus
> North Pole
> H0H 0H0
> Canada

In case you didn't notice, Santa's unique postal code **H0H 0H0** is extra special because it reads as "Ho ho ho!"

If you're in the US, this is the address you can send it to:

> Santa Claus
> 123 Elf Road
> North Pole, 88888
> U.S.A.

For those closer to the United Kingdom, you can send your letters to Father Christmas at:

> Santa/Father Christmas
> Santa's Grotto
> Reindeerland
> XM4 5HQ
> United Kingdom

If you're closer to Australia, here's his special mailing address:

Santa Claus
NORTH POLE 9999

No matter where you send it, he will get it, but please try and remember to put a stamp on it if you can. That helps it get delivered just a bit quicker.

santa speaks all languages

It doesn't matter what language you use to send your letters, Santa answers the letters in the same language in which they are sent. Some years, this means it's close to 200 different languages.

santa's magical reindeer

Among all of Santa's reindeer, Rudolph stands out with his luminous red nose, a beacon of light that guides Santa's sleigh on the cloudiest of nights. While the legends of reindeer have been told for centuries, the enchanting tale of Rudolph and his unique glow was brought to life by Robert L. May in 1939, adding an extra touch of magic to the Christmas narrative. Every year, Rudolph's story reminds us of the wonders of the season and the special place that even the most unexpected heroes can hold in our hearts.

The Names Of Santa's Reindeer: Santa's reindeer have become well-known thanks to Clement Clarke Moore's famous poem "A Visit from St. Nicholas" (commonly known as "The Night Before Christmas"). Their names are:

Dasher, Dancer, Prancer, Vixen, Comet, Cupid, Donner, Blitzen and Rudolph.

mystical reindeer power

Reindeer have long been associated with winter celebrations and Christmas joy. The idea of these magnificent creatures pulling Santa's sleigh has deep roots in Scandinavian folklore. Dating back centuries, these traditions weave a magical tale that captures the hearts of children and adults alike. Every Christmas Eve, the reindeer take their honored place in holiday legend, guiding Santa's sleigh through the night, a symbol of the season's enchantment and wonder.

reindeer noses are red, in infrared 🥶

Reindeer have numerous blood vessels in their noses that act as an internal heater and air conditioner, helping to regulate temperature not just in their nose, but in their brain. Using an infrared thermographic camera, all reindeer noses would appear red, not just the famous one of Rudolph.

all reindeer and caribou have antlers 🦌

Caribou and reindeer are the only species in the deer family where both males and the females have antlers.

The female's antlers are smaller than the males, but they carry them longer. Caribou and reindeer start growing their antlers in the spring. Males lose their antlers in late October/November. Females, especially those who have had babies, don't lose their antlers until May and June. This helps them protect their calves.

santa's reindeers are female

Since male reindeer shed their antlers in late October/November and female reindeer keep their antlers until after they give birth in the spring, any reindeer with antlers at Christmastime are likely to be female.

The clicking sound produced by reindeer as they walk results from the movement of tendons over their bones. Remarkably, reindeer can detect these clicks from several miles away. If one reindeer happens to fall behind or become separated from the herd, they can use these audible cues to navigate back and reunite with their group. It's this unique behavior that inspired the famous "click, click, click" lyrics found in the Christmas song 'Up On A Housetop.'

— Did Yule Know?!

---

tracking santa's flight 🎅

how norad's santa tracking started 🤙

The tradition of NORAD tracking Santa started in 1955 when the iconic American department store chain, Sears, misprinted a telephone number for children to call Santa in an advertisement. The number actually connected to the Continental Air Defense Command (CONAD), NORAD's predecessor.

Colonel Harry Shoup, who was on duty that night, answered the calls from children inquiring about Santa's whereabouts. Instead of dismissing them, he embraced the spirit and directed staff to provide updates on Santa's "flight."

operation santa claus 🦌

To carry on the tradition, NORAD launched "Operation Santa Claus" in 1958, a lighthearted way to keep children informed about Santa's journey on Christmas Eve. Today, NORAD uses advanced technology to track Santa's sleigh. This includes radar, satellites, high-speed digital cameras, and even fighter jets that "escort" Santa's sleigh as it enters North American airspace.

NORAD's Santa tracking requires a team of volunteers who dedicate their time to answering phone calls and providing updates to children around the world on Christmas Eve.

Over the years, NORAD's Santa tracking has grown immensely in popularity. In recent years, it's estimated that the program receives millions of calls and website visits from around the world.

Track Santa yourself at: www.noradsanta.org

global cooperation

NORAD's Santa tracking isn't limited to North America. It involves international cooperation with various organizations and even partner countries' air defense organizations.

google's interactive santa tracker

In 2004, Google launched its own festive interactive Santa tracker. Just like NORAD's Santa tracking, Google's Santa Tracker provides real-time updates on Santa's location as he travels from one destination to another.

What makes it different from NORAD's Santa tracking? Imagine Santa's journey fused with a magical journey of cultural discovery. With animated maps, playful games, and quizzes, you're not just tracking Santa; you're also diving into the holiday traditions of various countries.

To track Santa using Google's Santa tracker visit: santatracker. google.com

6
delectable delights

Christmas Foods & Drinks

Food plays a deliciously integral role in Christmas celebrations around the world, bringing families and communities together to savor festive flavors and honor age-old traditions. From mouthwatering feasts to delightful treats, each culture brings its unique culinary magic to the holiday table. Let's take a journey to explore some lesser-known fun facts about traditional Christmas foods that grace tables in different corners of the globe.

 Italy—Panettone's Rising Fame

Italy's beloved Panettone, a dome-shaped sweet bread, boasts origins dating back to the 15th century. Its name, "panettone," means "big loaf." But that's not all. Enter Pandoro, a golden, star-shaped cake that rivals Panettone's fame. And as families gather, the Feast of the Seven Fishes, "La Vigilia," graces the Christmas Eve spread, featuring an array of seafood dishes that honor Italian culinary tradition in all its flavorful glory.

🇲🇽 Mexico—Tamales with a Twist

Homemade corn and chicken tamales. Photo by bhofack2 via depositphotos.com

In Mexico, tamales are a Christmas staple. But did you know that some families hide a surprise within one tamale? Tradition holds that whoever finds a figurine of baby Jesus when unwrapping their tamale gets to host a gathering known as the "Día de la Candelaria," also known as Candlemas, on February 2nd, which marks the end of the Christmas season.

🇮🇸 Iceland—Fermented Festive Dish

Iceland serves up a unique holiday dish called "hákarl," a fermented shark. Prepared by burying the shark in sand and gravel for weeks, hákarl's distinctive aroma and flavor make it an acquired taste that might be best appreciated by adventurous eaters.

Japan—Kentucky Fried Chicken

While not a traditional Japanese holiday, Christmas has gained popularity in Japan as a time for gift-giving and feasting. Believe it or not, a bucket of fried chicken from the restaurant chain Kentucky Fried Chicken (KFC) has become a Japanese Christmas Eve tradition! It's so popular that orders are placed months in advance.

Greece—Reviving Christopsomo

Greek Christmas bread with walnuts. Photo by Author alexisdc via depositphotos.com

In Greece, "Christopsomo," or Christ's Bread, is a beautifully adorned, aromatic loaf baked with intricate designs or symbols. Traditionally, a cross and the family's initials are etched onto the bread before baking, signifying blessings and unity.

🇸🇪🍲Sweden—Creamy potato & fish casserole

In Sweden, a Christmas classic known as Jansson's Temptation, or 'Janssons frestelse' in Swedish, is a creamy potato and fish casserole. The fish used in the dish is called 'ansjovis,' which sounds like 'anchovies,' but isn't. It's actually spiced-cured sprat fillets. The recipe was first published in 1940 and quickly became a Swedish Christmas classic!

🇺🇦🍯 Ukraine—Kutia for Good Luck

Bowl of traditional kutia. Photo by Aw58, CC BY-SA 4.0 <https://creativecommons.org/licenses/by-sa/4.0>, via Wikimedia Commons

In Ukraine, "kutia" is a traditional Christmas dish made from wheat berries, poppy seeds, honey, nuts and dried fruits. An unusual custom involves families tossing a spoonful of kutia onto the ceiling. The more kernels that stick, the greater the fortune that's believed to come in the new year.

Portugal—The Diverse Bolo Rei

Traditional Bolo Rei cake. Photo by Zakharova via depositphotos.com

Portugal's "Bolo Rei" or "King Cake" is a festive dessert rich in symbolism. Hidden inside is a broad spectrum of surprises, including a dried fava bean and a figurine. The person who finds the bean might need to buy next year's cake, while the figurine symbolizes prosperity.

🇫🇮 Finland—Fisherman's Treasure

In Finland, "joulukinkku" is a traditional Christmas ham. This might be surprising considering Finland's abundance of lakes and access to fresh fish. That's why it's also common to serve fish dishes like "gravlax," which is raw salmon cured with sugar, salt, and dill.

🇬🇧 United Kingdom—Mince Pies

Mince pie. Photo by Jonathan Farber on Unsplash

Mince pies are a staple of British Christmas celebrations. Despite their name, they don't contain mince meat and often contain a mixture of sweet dried fruits and spices, making them a delightful treat.

🇪🇸 Spanish—Seafood Splurge

In Spain, "La Nochebuena" (Christmas Eve) is celebrated with a seafood feast. Dishes like shrimp, lobster, mussels, and clams are central to this lavish spread.

🏴🍞 Germany—Fruit Bread Flavors

Stollen, a fruit bread filled with nuts, spices, and candied fruit, and dusted with powdered sugar, is Germany's delectable addition to the global Christmas table.

🏴🍰 France—Bûche de Noël

Traditional Bûche de Noël or "Yule log" cake. Photo by NoirChocolate via depositphotos.com

The "Yule Log" cake, known as Bûche de Noël in French, is a rolled sponge cake often frosted and decorated to resemble a log. It's a popular dessert in France and other French-speaking countries.

🇺🇸 🇨🇦 🥛 United States & Canada—Eggnog

Eggnog, a creamy and spiced beverage made with eggs, milk, and often spiked with alcohol, is a classic holiday drink enjoyed in both the United States and Canada.

🇨🇦 🥧 Canada—Savory Tourtière

Traditional Tourtière, savory meat pie with buttery, flakey crust. Photo by elenathewise via depositphotos.com

In Québec and other parts of Canada, this savory double crusted meat pie is a special treat during the festive season. This traditional dish can be traced back to the 1600s when Québécois settlers attended midnight mass on Christmas Eve and then celebrated afterwards with a feast fit for a king, where Tourtière was always on the table.

Traditionally it was often made with wild game like rabbit, pheasant or moose. These days, there are several varieties, but the basic ingredients include a buttery pastry shell filled with spiced meats and vegetables, and then baked until the crust is golden and flaky. These four spices — cinnamon, clove, allspice and nutmeg — are almost always used and is what sets this meat pie apart from others.

Australia—Christmas BBQ

While many are wrapping up to stay warm, Aussies are firing up the barbecue! Christmas falls during their summer, so fresh seafood, steaks, and tropical fruits often grace their holiday tables.

Jamaica—Rich and Rummy Black Cake

In the Caribbean, especially in places like Jamaica, the traditional Christmas cake is a dense, dark cake filled with dried fruits and rum. It's a sweet, spirited treat enjoyed by many during the festive season.

South Africa—Tantalizing Trifle

In South Africa, Christmas wouldn't be complete without a trifle. This decadent dessert layers sponge cake, custard, jelly, and fruit. What's not so widely known is the touch of brandy or sherry that's often added to infuse the trifle with festive spirit.

Poland—The Wigilia Tradition

The traditional Polish Christmas Eve supper, known as Wigilia, features a grand spread of twelve different dishes, symbolizing the twelve apostles. No meat is consumed until the first star appears in the sky. One of these dishes is "barszcz wigilijny," a beet soup often served with mushroom-filled dumplings called "uszka."

🎴📦 Brazil—Rabanada's Hidden History

In Brazil, "rabanada" is a popular Christmas treat that resembles French toast. What's intriguing is that this dish has its roots in Portugal and was introduced to Brazil during the colonial period.

🏳️🔴 Hungary—Poppy Seed Goodness, Bejgli

Bejgli, traditional Hungarian poppy seed and walnut cake roll. Photo by accepto01 via depositphotos.com

A traditional Hungarian Christmas treat, this roll is packed with poppy seeds or walnuts and sweetened with honey and sugar, symbolizing hope and prosperity for the coming year.

🍹🌴 Caribbean Islands—Sip on Sorrel Drink

This bright red, spicy, and tangy drink is made from the petals of the sorrel flower, sweetened and flavored with ginger and cloves. Often, it's spiked with a touch of rum for an extra festive kick.

7
melodies of merriment

The Music of Christmas

L et the enchanting melodies of the season whisk you away as we delve into the 'Music of Christmas' in this chapter. From the timeless classics that warm our hearts to the surprising stories behind our favorite tunes, you're in for a musical sleigh ride like no other. Whether you're singing along to carols or rocking around the Christmas tree, this festive journey will have you tapping your toes and humming along to the holiday spirit!

songs & carols: the difference ♫♪

The terms "Christmas song" and "Christmas carol" are often used interchangeably, but there are subtle distinctions between the two.

Christmas carols and Christmas songs both celebrate the festive season, but they have distinct origins and themes. Carols, which have ancient roots, are primarily religious in nature and focus on the nativity story and events surrounding the birth of

Jesus. They've traditionally been sung in churches or by groups caroling door-to-door.

On the other hand, Christmas songs are a more recent tradition, emerging over the last century, and often highlight secular aspects of the holiday like Santa Claus, wintry scenes, and family gatherings.

While carols delve into the spiritual heart of Christmas, modern Christmas songs capture the broader festive ambiance of the season.

medieval merry-making 🍏

Wassailing and caroling are both festive traditions associated with the Christmas season, but they have distinct origins and meanings.

"Wassailing" originated in ancient England and initially involved toasting to good health with a mulled cider drink. Over time, it evolved to include singing to orchard trees for a bountiful harvest and later, house-to-house singing with an exchange of the wassail drink for gifts.

"Caroling," on the other hand, primarily refers to singing Christmas songs celebrating the birth of Jesus and related themes. While wassailing and caroling have intersected over the centuries, with some overlap in practices, they remain unique traditions with individual histories.

one of the first carols 👼

"Angels We Have Heard on High" is believed to be one of the earliest Christmas carols, with origins tracing back to France. It features joyful refrains and an exultant chorus that captures the spirit of the angels' proclamation.

shifting from pagan to christian

Many Christmas carols have roots in Pagan celebrations that were repurposed for Christian festivities. For example, "Deck the Halls" was originally a Welsh New Year's Eve carol. It later became associated with Christmas.

carols were once banned in england

Christmas carols, along with many other Christmas traditions, were effectively banned in England during the 17th century by the Puritans. This ban took place after the English Civil War, during the Interregnum period (1649-1660) when the Puritans and Oliver Cromwell, who was Lord Protector of the Commonwealth of England, Scotland, and Ireland, held power. The Puritans disapproved of celebrations and practices that they deemed to lack a biblical basis, including the celebration of Christmas and its associated customs.

Under Puritan rule, December 25th was treated as a regular working day, with festivities traditionally associated with Christmas, such as singing carols, being discouraged or even prohibited. Public observances related to Christmas were viewed unfavorably, as they were considered to be inconsistent with Puritan beliefs and practices.

The ban on Christmas celebrations, including caroling, was lifted with the restoration of the monarchy in 1660 when Charles II became king. However, it took time for many of the old customs, including the singing of carols, to gain widespread popularity again.

stories behind some of the most famous christmas songs and carols

silent night 🌙

The lyrics to this carol were penned by a young Austrian priest named Joseph Mohr in 1816, and the iconic melody was composed by a schoolteacher and organist named Franz Xaver Gruber. Mohr and Gruber debuted this carol together on Christmas Eve of 1818 at St. Nicholas Church in Oberndorf, Austria. Interestingly, the carol's creation was influenced by a damaged church organ, leading to its composition for guitar accompaniment.

"Silent Night" quickly transcended its origins, spreading internationally and capturing hearts around the world. It gained special significance during World War I when soldiers from opposing sides sang it together during a temporary truce. The carol's message of peace and unity resonates deeply. The carol's popularity has led to translations in countless languages, and its recognition as an intangible cultural heritage by UNESCO in 2011.

deck the halls 🎄

"Deck the Halls" is a Christmas carol that combines a traditional Welsh winter melody called "Nos Galan" with English lyrics that encourage decking the halls with holiday adorn-ments. Originating from the 16th century, the lively Welsh tune found new life when paired with lyrics in the late 19th century. The phrase "fa-la-la-la-la" is believed to be inspired by ancient medieval tunes known as "carols." The original Welsh lyrics celebrate the New Year rather than Christmas.

o holy night

"O Holy Night" originated in France as "Minuit, chrétiens" ("Midnight, Christians"). The lyrics were written by Placide Cappeau, a wine merchant, and poet, in 1847. Adolphe Adam, a French composer, set Cappeau's lyrics to music. Adam's composition beautifully complemented the poetic words and emotional theme of the carol. The carol was first performed on Christmas Eve in 1847 at the Church of St. Roch in Roque-maure, France. The soloist was the opera singer Emily Laurey.

At one point, "O Holy Night" was banned by French authori-ties due to its religious theme. However, its popularity was so immense that it couldn't be suppressed for long.

The English translation we know today was done by John Sullivan Dwight, an American music critic, in the mid-19th century. He aimed to capture the depth of the original French lyrics.

— Did Yule Know?!

carol of the bells ❀

"Carol of the Bells" has its roots in a Ukrainian folk song called "Shchedryk." The original song was not a Christmas carol but rather a New Year's chant that celebrated the coming of spring. The melody of "Carol of the Bells" was adapted by Ukrainian composer Mykola Leontovych in 1904. He was inspired by the sounds of ringing bells, and incorporated them into the song's arrangement. The carol gained popularity after it was performed by a choral group at the Kyiv University in Ukraine. The English lyrics were later added to the melody by Peter J. Wilhousky in the early 1930s. Wilhousky's version turned the song into the Christmas carol we know today, focusing on the joyful message of the holiday season.

o tannenbaum 🎄

"O Tannenbaum," also known as "O Christmas Tree," has an intriguing history that extends beyond its popular association with Christmas. Originally rooted in a 16th-century folk song, its modern form was shaped in 1824 by Ernst Anschütz, a Leipzig composer who transformed it into a song about a faithful evergreen tree.

Interestingly, the original German lyrics don't reference Christmas, focusing instead on the fir tree's symbol of steadfastness. The song has various versions in different languages, and its adaptation into "O Christmas Tree" in English significantly alters the original meaning.

"Tannenbaum" translates to "fir tree" in English.

jingle bells 🔔

James Lord Pierpont composed "Jingle Bells" in the mid-19th century, possibly around 1850, in Medford, Massachusetts. He wrote it for the children's Thanksgiving program at his father's church. Pierpont originally titled it "One Horse Open Sleigh."

The song was the first to be broadcast from space in a Christmas-themed prank by Gemini 6 astronauts in 1965.

white christmas ⛄

The same man that wrote "God Bless America," "There's No Business Like Show Business," and "Anything You Can Do," was the one to write one of the most famous Christmas songs of our time. Irving Berlin wrote "White Christmas" in 1940 while staying at the La Quinta Hotel in California. He was inspired by his own longing for the snowy Christmases of his childhood in New York.

Bing Crosby's rendition in the 1942 film *Holiday Inn* helped the song win the Academy Award for Best Original Song. The song's nostalgic lyrics resonated with soldiers during World War II, leading to its popularity and enduring appeal.

According to the Guinness Book of World Records, "White Christmas" is the *best-selling* Christmas song of all time, selling more than 50 million copies worldwide.

"White Christmas" has made an estimated $500 million in total earnings, making it the highest-grossing Christmas song of all time. It is estimated that it earns about $20 million per year in royalties. The Irving Berlin Music Company owns the copyright.

all i want for christmas is you

"All I Want for Christmas Is You" is considered the *most-played* Christmas song of all time, and it has become a global phenomenon. This instant classic, written and co-produced by Mariah Carey and Walter Afanasieff in 1994, was released as part of Mariah Carey's holiday album "Merry Christmas." It reportedly took the duo just 15 minutes to write the song.

"All I Want for Christmas Is You" has topped the charts in several countries and has earned Mariah Carey the title of "Queen of Christmas."

As of 2023, "All I Want for Christmas Is You" has sold around 19 million copies worldwide, and generated over $80 million in overall royalties. Mariah Carey and Walter Afanasieff enjoy the lion's share of that revenue. It is estimated that Carey makes around $2.5 million per year from "All I Want for Christmas Is You". This number is likely to increase in the coming years, as the song continues to grow in popularity.

rudolph the red-nosed reindeer

The magical story and character of Rudolph the red-nosed reindeer was created in 1939 by Robert L. May as a promotional holiday booklet for the American department store, Montgomery Ward. A decade after the booklet was released, May's famous song-writing brother-in-law, Jonny Marks, adapted the story into a song. Gene Autry's recording of the song in 1949 became a best-seller, and the character Rudolph quickly became a beloved holiday icon.

Rudolph is one of the few reindeer whose name and even likeness are trademarked. The Rudolph Company, set up by Robert L. May before he died in 1976, owns the trademark to Rudolph.

— Did Yule Know?!

feliz navidad 🐱

Puerto Rican musician José Feliciano wrote and released "Feliz Navidad" in 1970, blending English and Spanish lyrics in a cheerful holiday greeting. José Feliciano's intention was to create a song that would bring joy to people of various cultures, making it a festive cross-cultural celebration.

"Feliz Navidad" has been covered by numerous artists in different languages and styles, further popularizing the song and ensuring its continued presence during the holiday season. It has been translated into various languages, including French, German, Italian, and Japanese.

last christmas 🎵

"Last Christmas" was released by the British duo Wham! in 1984 as a single. It quickly became a massive hit and remains one of the most iconic Christmas songs of all time. Despite its upbeat melody, the lyrics reflect themes of lost love and bitter-sweet memories, making it a unique addition to the holiday playlist.

happy xmas (war is over)

The song was written by John Lennon and Yoko Ono in 1971. It was inspired by Lennon's and Ono's desire to create a song that would promote peace and understanding during the Christmas season. Although the song didn't initially become a huge hit upon its release, it has gained immense popularity over the years and is now considered a Christmas classic.

John Lennon and Yoko Ono agreed to donate all of the song's proceeds to UNICEF. This agreement still stands today, and the song continues to raise money for UNICEF's important work across nations. UNICEF is a United Nations agency that improves the lives of children around the world. Their work includes providing food, water, healthcare, education, and protection to children in need. UNICEF has helped millions of children over the years, and the song "Happy Xmas (War Is Over)" has played a small role in their work.

fairytale of new york

In the United Kingdom, this song is often voted as the nation's favorite Christmas song. "Fairytale of New York" is a beloved Christmas song by The Pogues, featuring Kirsty MacColl, and it's known for its unique blend of music styles and heartfelt storytelling.

The Pogues, known for their punk rock roots, teamed up with folk singer Kirsty MacColl to create a distinctive fusion of Irish folk and rock in "Fairytale of New York."

The song's lyrics tell a raw and unfiltered story of a troubled relationship, portraying a less conventional and sometimes gritty view of the holiday season. Some UK radio stations have chosen to play edited versions or have banned the song entirely, due to concerns over the lyrics. The controversy centers around specific words in the lyrics that are considered offensive and derogatory, particularly a homophobic slur.

we wish you a merry christmas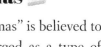

The origin of "We Wish You a Merry Christmas" is believed to date back to 16th-century England. It emerged as a type of wassailing song, sung by carolers who went door-to-door to offer good wishes and request treats from wealthy households.

The song's lyrics reflect the wassailing tradition, where the singers express their good wishes for a joyful Christmas and anticipate receiving something in return. The line "Now bring us some figgy pudding" is a nod to the tradition of requesting treats like pudding or other festive foods.

"Figgy pudding," also called "plum pudding," or "Christmas pudding" is a traditional Christmas dessert from England. Figs are sometimes included. The term "plum" in "plum pudding" historically referred to various dried fruits, such as raisins or currants, rather than actual plums. The mixture might include a variety of dried fruits, spices, suet (a type of animal fat), breadcrumbs, treacle or molasses, and brandy. The pudding is traditionally made well in advance of Christmas, sometimes even a year ahead, allowing the flavors to develop and mature.

On Christmas Day, the pudding is theatrically set ablaze with more brandy, creating a spectacular blue flame, a ritual symbolizing Christ's passion and adding a unique caramelized flavor. Accompanying this show-stopper are brandy butter, a sweet, rich blend of butter and brandy, and a smooth, creamy custard, both enhancing the pudding's intense flavors.

— Did Yule Know?!

---

the 12 days of christmas 🌳

"The Twelve Days of Christmas" is a traditional English Christmas carol with an origin dating back several centuries. The song is structured around the concept of the "Twelve Days of Christmas," a period that begins on December 25 (Christmas Day) and ends on January 5, also known as Twelfth Night.

The song is a cumulative counting song, where each verse introduces a new gift given by "my true love" on each of the twelve days. The list of gifts is repeated and expanded with each new verse. The gifts are often interpreted as symbols, with hidden meanings related to Christian teachings.

The exact origin of "The Twelve Days of Christmas" is a bit mysterious, but it's believed to have evolved over time through oral tradition and variations in lyrics. The earliest known printed version of the song appeared in the book "Mirth Without Mischief" in the 1780s, but the song's history likely predates this publication.

joy to the world 🎺

"Joy to the World" was not originally written as a Christmas song. The lyrics were actually penned by English hymn writer Isaac Watts in 1719 as a hymn celebrating the second coming of Jesus Christ. The melody commonly associated with "Joy to the World" was composed by Lowell Mason in the 19th century. He adapted the melody from a section of George Frideric Handel's composition "Messiah."

While "Joy to the World" is a beloved Christmas hymn, its lyrics are focused on Christ's triumphant return rather than his nativity. Despite this, the song's joyful and uplifting tone makes it a popular choice for Christmas celebrations.

the christmas song (chestnuts roasting on an open fire) 🌰

"The Christmas Song" was written by Mel Tormé and Bob Wells on a hot summer day in 1945. They were inspired to write about winter and Christmas to cool off! Mel Tormé wrote the music in just 40 minutes. The original title of the song was "Merry Christmas to You."

Nat King Cole created a recording of the song in 1946. But the version of "The Christmas Song" by Nat King Cole that is most commonly heard on the radio and during the holiday season is his 1961 re-recording. That recording, known as the "chestnuts roasting" version, was recorded for his album "The Nat King Cole Story," and is the rendition that has become an iconic and timeless classic.

rockin' around the christmas tree

"Rockin' Around the Christmas Tree" is one of the most popular Christmas songs of all time. It was written by Jewish songwriter Johnny Marks, who also wrote the song, "Rudolph the Red-Nosed Reindeer" and "A Holly Jolly Christmas".

It was first recorded by Brenda Lee in 1958, when she was only 13 years old. It was released in 1958, but didn't become a hit until 1960. The song was made known to a new generation when it was used in the hit 1990 movie, *Home Alone*. Brenda performs "Rockin'" at all of her concerts, no matter what time of year and considers it her signature song.

The song has been covered by over 100 artists, including Miley Cyrus, Carrie Underwood, and Meghan Trainor. It's also been translated into over 20 languages.

greatest holiday songs of all time

According to Billboard, Rolling Stone, and the Official Charts Company, these are the top ten Christmas songs in the U.S.:

1. "All I Want for Christmas Is You" - *Mariah Carey* (1994)
2. "Rockin' Around the Christmas Tree" - *Brenda Lee* (1958)
3. "Jingle Bell Rock" - *Bobby Helms* (1957)
4. "The Christmas Song (Merry Christmas to You)" - *Nat King Cole* (1960)
5. "A Holly Jolly Christmas" - *Burl Ives* (1965)

6. "Feliz Navidad" - *Jose Feliciano* (1970)
7. "It's the Most Wonderful Time of the Year" - *Andy Williams* (1963)
8. "Last Christmas" - *Wham!* (1984)
9. "Let It Snow, Let It Snow, Let It Snow" - *Dean Martin* (1959)
10. "White Christmas" - *Bing Crosby* (1947)

the five most hated christmas songs

According to a survey by YouGov in 2021, the top five most hated Christmas songs in the U.S. are:

1. "Santa Baby" – *Eartha Kitt with Henri René and His Orchestra* (1953)
2. "Grandma Got Run Over by a Reindeer" – *Elmo & Patsy* (1979)
3. "I Saw Mommy Kissing Santa Claus" – *Jimmy Boyd* (1952)
4. "Wonderful Christmastime" – *Paul McCartney* (1979)
5. "Baby, It's Cold Outside" – *Dean Martin & Cyd Chadrisse* (1949)

The survey polled 1,000 Americans and asked them to rate their dislike of 20 Christmas songs on a scale of 1 to 5, with 1 being "dislike very much" and 5 being "like very much." The songs were then ranked by their average score.

Here are some of the reasons why people might hate these songs:

- "Grandma Got Run Over by a Reindeer" is often considered to be a dark and morbid song. The lyrics tell the story of a grandmother who is accidentally run over by a reindeer on Christmas Eve.
- "I Saw Mommy Kissing Santa Claus" is a song about a child who witnesses their mother kissing Santa Claus. Some people find the song to be creepy or inappropriate.
- "Wonderful Christmastime" is a song that is often criticized for being too repetitive and catchy. Some people find the song to be annoying.
- "Baby, It's Cold Outside" is a song that portrays a conversation between a couple debating whether the woman should stay the night. In the lyrics, the woman expresses a desire to leave, while the man persistently urges her to stay, including a controversial line that implies he may have spiked her drink. This aspect of the song has led some listeners to view it as suggestive or outdated.

8

christmas in space

Extraterrestrial Celebrations

Prepare **to leave Earth behind** and venture into the cosmos for a truly out-of-this-world Christmas experience! In this chapter, we're strapping on our space helmets and joining astronauts on the International Space Station (ISS) to explore the unique and exhilarating ways they celebrate the holiday season in microgravity.

deck the hull: xmas in zero gravity 🚀

Decorating for Christmas takes on a whole new dimension in space. With no gravity to ground them, ornaments and stockings float freely, creating a mesmerizing display of holiday cheer. Astronauts creatively repurpose everyday items to craft festive decorations that celebrate the spirit of the season.

Fun Fact: On the ISS, astronauts often use Velcro, tape, and other adhesives to keep decorations in place. These innovative solutions ensure that even in microgravity, Christmas magic is alive and well.

santa's sleigh: treats & goodies 🍗

What's Christmas without a feast of traditional holiday treats? Astronauts aboard the ISS enjoy specially packaged meals that include turkey, cranberry sauce, and other festive fare. While the lack of gravity makes eating a unique experience, the camaraderie and shared meals create a sense of togetherness reminiscent of holiday gatherings on Earth.

Fun Fact: To ensure that food remains contained and doesn't float away, astronauts use containers with lids and pouches when they eat. They also use tortillas instead of bread for sandwiches.

two christmases on the iss 🛰️

The crews onboard the ISS celebrate Christmas at two different times. Most astronauts celebrate on December 25th. But the Russians celebrate the Orthodox Christmas, which falls on January 7th.

There's a box of Christmas decorations on the ISS that crews use to make the place feel more festive around the holidays. The decorations include plastic strings of lights, Santa hats, Christmas stockings and a Christmas tree just a little over one foot tall.

holiday shopping a year in advance

Clothes and other personal items are often sent to the space station months before the crew actually arrive onboard. If you wanted to share gifts with your crewmates or get matching festive pajamas, you'd have to think a year or more in advance to make sure you purchase, pack and get them "shipped" in time.

space stockings: gifts & surprises 🎁

Expedition 16 crew celebrating Christmas onboard the ISS. Left to Right: cosmonaut Yuri I. Malenchenko, astronaut Peggy A. Whitson, and astronaut Daniel Tani. *Photo courtesy of NASA.*

Just like on Earth, stockings are hung with care on the ISS. Astronauts receive care packages from family and friends, complete with handwritten notes, photographs, and small trinkets. The joy of unwrapping these gifts amid the vastness of space adds an extra layer of warmth and connection.

Fun Fact: Because weight is a precious resource in space, even the smallest gifts are cherished. Astronauts often exchange practical items like socks, snacks, and personal care products.

silent night: finding peace in space

Amid the hustle and bustle of daily life on the ISS, astronauts seek moments of tranquility during the holiday season. Gazing out at the breathtaking views of Earth from space, they find solace and a sense of wonder that transcends language and borders.

Fun Fact: Onboard the ISS, night changes to day and back again every 45 minutes due to the station's orbit around Earth. This unique cycle allows astronauts to witness 16 sunrises and sunsets in a single day!

embracing diversity in space

Astronauts on the ISS come from diverse cultures and backgrounds, each bringing their own holiday traditions and customs. Christmas in space becomes a celebration of unity and shared experiences, where astronauts learn about and embrace the festivities of their colleagues from around the world.

Fun Fact: While Christmas is widely celebrated, other religious and cultural holidays are also acknowledged and respected on the ISS. This diversity fosters a sense of harmony and mutual understanding among the crew.

8 holidays a year!

Astronauts aboard the International Space Station (ISS) are allotted the opportunity to celebrate up to eight holidays each year, although individual crews are typically on board for six months. Before their mission, each crew decides on four holidays they will observe during their stay, drawing from a diverse array of traditions including American, Russian, European, Japanese, and Canadian celebrations. Possible choices include Thanksgiving, France's Bastille Day, Russian Cosmonaut Day on April 12th, Halloween, Easter, Hanukkah, and Ramadan. Sharing and experiencing these international holidays together is often a highlight and fond memory for the crew members.

special meals & calling home

For holidays, the international crews will share a special meal together and then call home to talk to friends, family, and other loved ones.

9
christmas traditions around the world

This holiday season, journey across continents to explore unique Christmas greetings and traditions from around the world. From the heartwarming King or Queen's Christmas Message in the UK to Ukraine's special festive spider webs, discover the diverse ways people celebrate this joyous occasion.

christmas greetings 🎅

In different parts of the world, different cultures use different ways of wishing each other holiday cheer. Here are a few examples:

🇬🇧 United Kingdom

In the United Kingdom, people typically say "Happy Christmas." The phrase "Happy Christmas" is thought to have originated in the 16th century.

🏴 🍁 United States & Canada

In the United States and Canada, people typically say "Merry Christmas" or "Happy Holidays." The phrase "Merry Christmas" is thought to have originated in the 17th century. The phrase "Happy Holidays" is a more secular greeting that is often used to avoid offending people who do not celebrate Christmas.

If you're in Hawaii, you'll hear "Mele Kalikimaka." It's a mix of Hawaiian and English, and it's a tropical way of saying "Merry Christmas."

Did Yule Know?!

🇲🇽 Mexico

In Mexico, people typically say "Feliz Navidad" (pronounced "feh-leeth nah-vee-dad") or "Merry Christmas." The phrase "Feliz Navidad" is Spanish for "Merry Christmas."

🇦🇺 Australia

In Australia, people typically say "Merry Christmas" or "Season's Greetings." The phrase "Season's Greetings" is a more general greeting that is used to wish someone well during the holiday season.

🇳🇿 New Zealand

In New Zealand, people typically say "Merry Christmas" or "Māori Christmas." Māori Christmas is a celebration of Christmas that combines traditional Māori customs with Christian traditions.

▉▉ Italy

In Italy, people say "Buon Natale" (pronounced "bwon nah-tee-leh"). This also literally means "Merry Christmas" in Italian.

▉▉France

In France, people say "Joyeux Noël" (pronounced "zhwa-yuh no-el"). This literally means "Merry Christmas" in French.

▉ Germany

In Germany, people say "Frohe Weihnachten" (pronounced "fro-huh vey-nahkh-ten"). This also literally means "Merry Christmas" in German.

a time-honored tradition 👑

In the United Kingdom, a cherished Christmas tradition transcends homes and gathers the nation around its screens. The annual King or Queen's Christmas Message has been an integral part of British Christmases for decades, offering a unique blend of royal insight, reflection, and unity.

This heartfelt address, which is usually broadcast on Christmas Day, was started by King George V in 1932 with a simple radio broadcast. Since then, it has evolved with the times, embracing television and digital platforms, ensuring that the royal message reaches people across the realm and beyond.

The King or Queen's Christmas Message is an opportunity for the monarch to reflect on the year gone by, offering words of comfort, encouragement, and inspiration. It often addresses themes of hope, community, and the enduring values that hold society together. The message carries a unifying tone, reminding everyone of the importance of compassion and shared values, particularly during the festive season.

First Televised Message: Queen Elizabeth II delivered the first televised Christmas Message in 1957, allowing the public to see and hear their monarch during the festive season.

Personal Touch: The message often features personal anecdotes from the monarch's own experiences, creating a relatable and empathetic connection with the public.

Common Themes: Over the years, the message has often focused on unity, peace, compassion, and hope, resonating with people during times of joy and challenges alike.

Global Reach: The message isn't just for the UK—thanks to digital technology, people around the world can tune in and share in the festive spirit.

Interfaith Embrace: The message acknowledges the diverse faiths within the UK, emphasizing the importance of unity and respect for different cultures and beliefs.

Location Variety: Queen Elizabeth II delivered her Christmas message from various locations, including Buckingham Palace, Windsor Castle, and even the Antarctic.

united kingdom's pantomimes 🇬🇧

From boisterous audience engagement to witty humor and enchanting performances, pantomimes are a cherished Christmas tradition that brings joy and laughter to audiences of all ages across the UK.

Pantomimes, or "pantos," are lively and interactive stage shows held during the Christmas season in the UK. They combine elements of comedy, music, dance, and audience participation.

Traditional Roots: Pantomimes have their origins in 16th-century Italian "Commedia dell'arte" theater, known for its stock characters and slapstick humor.

Famous Characters: Pantomimes feature a range of iconic characters, including the principal boy (played by a woman), the dame (played by a man in a flamboyant female costume), and the villain.

Fairy Tale Twist: Pantomimes often revolve around well-known fairy tales, such as "Cinderella," "Aladdin," "Snow White," and "Jack and the Beanstalk," adding a creative twist to the stories.

Audience Interaction: One of the most enjoyable aspects of pantomimes is the encouragement of audience participation. Audiences are encouraged to cheer, boo, and shout out traditional phrases like "He's Behind You!," creating an energetic atmosphere.

Spectacular Costumes: Lavish and colorful costumes are a hallmark of pantos. The dame's outfits are often especially extravagant and hilarious.

The Dame Character: The dame is typically portrayed by a male actor dressed in flamboyant and exaggerated female clothing. This character is a comedic figure who adds humor and entertainment to the pantomime. The tradition of having a male actor play the dame dates back to the origins of pantomime in the 18th century, and is an integral part of the pantomime.

Catchy Songs: Pantomimes feature popular songs and musical numbers that are often rewritten with humorous lyrics related to the plot. Here are some fun examples:

Original Song: "Shape of You" by Ed Sheeran
Pantomime Version for 'Aladdin':

> *"So come on now, follow me, through Agrabah's*
> *   streets,*
> *Every day discovering something brand new,*
> *Oh I'm in love with my magic shoe."*

Original Song: "Can't Stop the Feeling!" by Justin Timberlake
Pantomime Version for 'Cinderella':

> *"I got this feeling in my bones,*
> *Gotta make it to the ball before it's gone,*
> *All through my city, all through my home,*
> *Fairy godmother's on the phone."*

Original Song: "Uptown Funk" by Mark Ronson ft. Bruno Mars
Pantomime Version for 'Jack and the Beanstalk':

"Uptown Beanstalk, gonna climb you up,
Uptown Beanstalk, reach the clouds above!"

Original Song: "Bad Guy" by Billie Eilish
Pantomime Version for 'Snow White':

"I'm the bad queen,
Duh!
I like it when you take a bite,
Of my poisoned apple, make it night."

Original Song: "Happy" by Pharrell Williams
Pantomime Version for 'Peter Pan':

"Because I fly,
Clap along if you feel like Neverland's the truth,
Clap along if you know Tinkerbell's on the roof."

Topical Humor: Pantomimes incorporate current events and pop culture references, making each performance relevant and engaging for the audience.

Star-Studded Casts: Many pantomime productions feature well-known actors, singers, and celebrities, making them a star-studded affair. Some examples include:

- **Sir Ian McKellen:** The renowned actor, famous for roles in "The Lord of the Rings" and "X-Men," played Widow Twankey in "Aladdin" at the Old Vic Theatre in London.
- **Henry Winkler:** Best known as "The Fonz" in "Happy Days," Winkler has played Captain Hook in "Peter Pan" in various UK pantomimes.

- **David Hasselhoff:** The "Baywatch" and "Knight Rider" star has appeared in several pantomimes, including roles as Captain Hook and Hoff the Hook.
- **Craig Revel Horwood:** The "Strictly Come Dancing" judge has appeared in various pantos, often as a villain, such as the Wicked Queen in "Snow White."
- **Pamela Anderson:** The "Baywatch" actress made her pantomime debut as the Genie of the Lamp in "Aladdin" at the New Wimbledon Theatre.

Local Productions: While major theaters in cities like London host grand pantomime productions, smaller theaters and communities across the UK also put on their own delightful shows.

Unexpected Twists: Pantomimes are known for their unexpected and humorous twists, ensuring that even familiar stories have surprising elements.

Limited Time: Pantomimes typically run during the holiday season, starting in November and extending into January, offering a festive entertainment option.

Diverse Appeal: Pantomimes are suitable for all audiences, making them a perfect outing for families, friends, and even groups of coworkers.

Supporting Theaters: Pantomimes often generate a significant portion of revenue for theaters, supporting their operations and allowing them to offer more performances throughout the year.

iceland's book flood 🇮🇸 📖

Jólabókaflóð, also known as the "Christmas Book Flood," is a heartwarming and unique tradition that takes place in Iceland during the holiday season. This Icelandic tradition combines the joy of giving and receiving books with the cozy comfort of spending quality time with loved ones.

World War II Origins: The tradition originated during World War II, when paper was one of the few resources not in short supply due to the island's isolation. As a result, giving books as gifts became a popular choice. Over the years, this practice evolved into a beloved cultural tradition that promotes reading and literature.

Christmas Eve Gift Exchange & Reading: The Jólabókaflóð celebration begins on Christmas Eve, when families exchange books as gifts. This thoughtful gesture encourages the joy of reading and the sharing of stories. People of all ages receive books, from children to adults, making this a truly inclusive tradition that values the importance of literacy and learning.

After the book exchange, families gather together to read their newly received books. As people dive into the pages of their new books, the cozy atmosphere is further enhanced by the tradition of enjoying warm beverages such as hot cocoa. This intimate and peaceful evening of reading fosters a sense of togetherness and creates lasting memories for families and friends.

Read for a Few Hours or Read All Night: The idea of

staying up all night to read is not a strict rule, but rather a cultural practice that has developed over time. Some people may choose to read for only a few hours, while others might stay up late into the night.

Growing International Popularity: Jólabókaflóð has gained international recognition as a heartwarming example of a holiday tradition that promotes literature and quality time spent with loved ones. It reflects Iceland's deep appreciation for books and its commitment to maintaining a high level of literacy among its population. The tradition's emphasis on the joy of reading, coupled with the comfort of being surrounded by family, encapsulates the true spirit of the holiday season in Iceland.

Iceland is known for its exceptionally high literacy rates. The tradition of exchanging books during Jólabókaflóð has played a role in fostering a culture of reading and learning. This tradition has contributed to Iceland's reputation as a country with a strong literary heritage.

— Did Yule Know?!

ukraine's special festive spider webs

In Ukraine, Christmas is a significant holiday celebrated with various unique customs and traditions. One of the most intriguing traditions involves decorating Christmas trees with spider webs made from silver or gold thread.

The Tale of the Christmas Spider: This tradition is rooted in a folktale about a poor widow and her children who woke up on Christmas morning to find their tree covered in spider webs that turned into silver and gold as the sun shone on them.

Spreading Good Luck: The spider web decorations are believed to bring good luck and prosperity to the household for the coming year.

Unique Tree Decorations: Ukrainian families combine spider webs with traditional ornaments like colorful beads, paper chains, and straw decorations, creating a one-of-a-kind festive look.

Celebrating Simplicity: The tradition emphasizes finding beauty and wonder in even the simplest of circumstances, making it a heartwarming symbol of the Christmas spirit.

spain's christmas lottery & "el gordo" 💰

The Spanish Christmas Lottery has been held annually since 1812, making it one of the world's oldest continuous lotteries. It has become an integral part of Spain's holiday season.

El Gordo: The highlight of the Spanish Christmas Lottery is the "El Gordo" (The Fat One) prize, which is one of the largest single payout lottery prizes in the world. It can bring life-changing sums of money to the winners.

Prizes: There are thousands of prizes available, ensuring many winners. The grand prize, "El Gordo," is a significant amount but is just one of the many prizes. This design means that the prize pool is spread among a larger number of participants.

Odds: Compared to many other major lotteries worldwide, the odds of winning a prize in the Spanish Christmas Lottery are quite favorable, given the large number of total prizes.

Elaborate Drawing Ceremony: The drawing of the lottery takes place on December 22nd each year. The event is broadcasted live on television and radio, and it features school children singing the winning numbers in a traditional and theatrical manner.

Supporting Good Causes: A portion of the lottery proceeds goes towards funding various charitable causes in Spain, making it a way for participants to contribute to social initiatives while also having a chance to win.

germany's hidden pickle ornament

Hiding a pickle ornament in the Christmas tree is known as the "Christmas Pickle" tradition, and is popular in some parts of Germany and the United States.

Origins: The exact origin of the Christmas Pickle tradition is debated, and there are a few different stories that claim to explain its beginnings. One popular story suggests that the tradition comes from Germany in the late 19th century.

According to this story, a pickle was hidden in the Christmas tree, and the child who found it first received an extra gift or was said to have good luck for the coming year. Some variations of the story also claim that the pickle finder would get to open the first gift.

How it Works: In households that follow this tradition, a pickle-shaped ornament is hidden somewhere in the Christmas tree after it's fully decorated. The ornament is often green and blends in with the tree's branches, making it a bit challenging to spot. On Christmas morning, the children in the family embark on a search to find the hidden pickle ornament.

Prize and Fun: The child who finds the pickle ornament is typically awarded a small gift, treat, or even the honor of opening the first present. The tradition adds an element of excitement and friendly competition to the holiday celebration, as everyone searches for the hidden pickle. It's not uncommon for adults to join in the fun as well.

Variations: While the tradition is most associated with Germany, it has also become popular in some parts of the United States, particularly in areas with strong German-American communities. However, it's worth noting that the Christmas Pickle tradition is not universally known or practiced, even within these countries.

10
christmas legends from around the world

S tep into a world where folklore and festivity collide! In this chapter, we'll journey through the captivating realm of Christmas legends and myths. These timeless tales have been passed down through generations, enriching the holiday season with a touch of magic, mystery, and a hint of the unknown. From the boisterous Krampus of Austria to the mischievous Tomte of Scandinavia, let's explore the fascinating characters and creatures that make Christmas even more enchanting.

krampus: the dark side of yuletide 👹

Venture into the Alpine regions of Austria and Bavaria, where the legend of Krampus reigns supreme. Often portrayed as a horned and fearsome creature, Krampus is the yin to Santa's yang. While Santa rewards good children, Krampus punishes the naughty ones.

Krampus' punishments can range from mild pranks and scaring misbehaving kids to more severe actions, like kidnapping or whipping them with birch branches.

This ancient tradition of celebrating both light and dark adds a thrilling twist to the season of giving.

People dressed as Krampus. Photo by budabar via depositphotos.com

Fun Fact: In some European towns, people participate in Krampusnacht, a lively parade where performers dress up as Krampus and roam the streets, delighting and sometimes terrifying the onlookers.

tomte: guardians of the homestead 🧝

Across the snowy landscapes of Scandinavia, a tiny but mighty guardian roams. Meet the Tomte, a mythical creature resembling a gnome or elf. Tomte are believed to watch over homes, barns, and farms, ensuring good fortune and protection for the inhabitants. Leave a bowl of porridge out on Christmas Eve, and the Tomte might just bring blessings in return.

Fun Fact: The Tomte is closely related to other folkloric beings like the Nisse in Denmark and Norway, and the Tonttu in Finland. Despite regional variations, these creatures share the common role of benevolent household spirits.

la befana: italy's christmas witch

In Italy, Christmas wouldn't be complete without the tale of La Befana. Legend has it that after initially declining the invitation of the Three Wise Men to visit the baby Jesus, La Befana had a change of heart. Regretting her decision, she embarked on a lifelong quest to find the Christ child, flying on her broomstick. On the night of Epiphany Eve (January 5th) she visits children's homes, leaving gifts and sweets for those who have been good and a lump of coal, an onion, or dark candy for those who have been naughty.

La Befana. Naturpuur, CC BY 4.0, via Wikimedia Commons

La Befana is a kind-hearted, but quirky witch who is typically portrayed as an old woman, often depicted with a long, crooked nose, a shawl, and a broomstick. She is sometimes referred to as the "Christmas Witch" or the "Good Witch."

While milk and cookies are left for Babbo Natale, wine and local sweet treats, like a slice of panettone or a regional pastry, is left for La Befana.

Fun Fact: In Italy, Epiphany, or "La Festa dell'Epifania," which falls on January 6th, is a significant holiday that marks the culmination of the Christmas season. La Befana's arrival is met with celebrations, parades, and festive gatherings.

mari lwyd: wales' festive horse skull

A Mari Lwyd horse skull with ribbons and bells. Photo by R. fiend, CC BY-SA 3.0, via Wikimedia Commons

In some villages of Wales, a peculiar tradition known as Mari Lwyd comes to life. A horse skull adorned with ribbons and bells is paraded through the streets, accompanied by singing and merriment. This ancient custom, with roots in pre-Christian times, adds a touch of whimsy and intrigue to the Yuletide season.

Fun Fact: Mari Lwyd celebrations involve "pwnco," a rhyming exchange of verses between the horse party and the household they visit. This playful banter is an essential part of the tradition.

frau holle: germany's snow queen 🇩🇪

In German folklore, Frau Holle, or Mother Hulda, presides over winter and snow. Legend has it that her actions influence the weather, and her presence is celebrated during the winter months. The story of a kind-hearted girl's encounter with Frau Holle emphasizes the virtues of hard work and compassion.

Fun Fact: The tale of Frau Holle has regional variations across Germany, but the central theme of rewarding industriousness remains constant. The story's influence is woven into Christmas customs and celebrations.

iceland's gryla & the yule lads 🇮🇸

Iceland has a group of 13 mischievous Yule Lads who visit children during the 13 nights leading up to Christmas. Each Yule Lad has a distinct personality and behavior, ranging from leaving gifts to playing pranks. Children leave their shoes on windowsills, and depending on their behavior, the Yule Lads either reward them with small gifts or rotten potatoes.

The Yule Lads are the offspring of Gryla, a fearsome troll who kidnaps and cooks misbehaving children in a stew. Gryla is often accompanied by the Yule Cat, creating a duo that encourages children to be on their best behavior during the holiday season.

Fun Fact: Among the Yule Lads, there are some with rather peculiar names and behaviors. "Window Peeper" is known for peering into windows to spot potential gifts, while "Door Sniffer" has an extraordinary sense of smell and can sniff out food from afar.

netherlands & belgium's zwarte piet

Also known as "Black Pete," Zwarte Piet is a traditional figure in Dutch and Belgian Christmas traditions. Zwarte Piet is said to be a helper of Sinterklaas (St. Nicholas) and is often portrayed with a dark complexion and colorful clothing. Zwarte Piet is known for leaving gifts, candies, and treats in children's shoes that are placed near the fireplace or window. This tradition is a highlight of the Sinterklaas celebration and is eagerly anticipated by young children.

Fun Fact: In 2013, UNESCO recognized the Sinterklaas festivities, including the character of Zwarte Piet, as part of the Intangible Cultural Heritage of Humanity.

11
other winter holidays

Embracing Diversity

Christmas is a popular holiday celebrated around the world, but it's not the only winter celebration. In fact, there are many other winter holidays celebrated by different cultures, each with its own unique traditions and customs.

In this chapter, we'll take a look at some of the most popular winter celebrations from around the world. We'll learn about their history, their significance, and some of the fun facts that make them so special.

hanukkah - festival of lights 🕎

While Christmas and Hanukkah are distinct celebrations, both share a spirit of warmth, love, and community during the holiday season. This Jewish holiday celebrates the rededication of the Second Temple in Jerusalem. It is celebrated for eight days, beginning on the 25th day of Kislev on the Hebrew calendar.

Celebrating the rededication of the Second Temple in Jerusalem. The rededication of the Second Temple is a significant event in Jewish history. The temple was destroyed by the Babylonians in 586 BCE, and it was not rebuilt until 19 BCE. The rededication of the temple was a time of great joy and celebration for the Jewish people.

Hanukkah Dates. Hanukkah does not have a fixed date on the Gregorian calendar. Instead, it falls on different dates each year in late November to late December, aligning with the Hebrew calendar. The holiday begins on the 25th of Kislev and lasts for eight days.

Hanukkah is celebrated for eight days, starting on the 25th of Kislev. Hanukkah is celebrated for eight days because there was only enough oil to light the menorah for one day, but it miraculously lasted for eight days. This miracle is a reminder of God's power and protection.

Lighting the menorah using the shamash. Photo VadimVasenin by via depositphotos.com

The main symbol of Hanukkah is the menorah, a nine-branched candelabra. The menorah is a nine-branched candelabra that is lit during Hanukkah. The first candle is lit on the first night of Hanukkah, and an additional candle is lit each night until all eight candles, plus the shamash (helper candle), are lit on the final night. The menorah is a symbol of the rededication of the Second Temple and the miracle of the oil.

The Shamash, The ninth candle is called the "shamash," meaning "servant" or "helper" in Hebrew. This candle is used to light the other eight candles and is typically placed at a different height or position from the others to distinguish it. The shamash is lit first, and then used to light the other candles, adding one more candle each night of Hanukkah, from right to left, but lighting them from left to right (newest to oldest).

The presence of the shamash serves both a practical and symbolic purpose. Practically, it provides a source of light, since the other candles are considered sacred and are not supposed to be used for mundane activities like lighting each other or illuminating a room. Symbolically, the shamash represents service and leadership, as it is the candle that "serves" the others.

Spelling Variations: The spelling of Hanukkah can vary due to transliteration from Hebrew to English. You may come across different spellings such as Hanukah, Chanukah, or even other variations. The variation in spelling adds to the richness and diversity of the holiday's celebration worldwide.

Hanukkah and Christmas Overlap: Occasionally, Hanukkah and Christmas coincide, leading to the playful term "Chrismukkah" or "Hanumas." This blending of traditions acknowledges the celebration of both holidays in interfaith families or communities.

One of the most popular Hanukkah foods is latkes, which are potato pancakes. Latkes are potato pancakes that are traditionally eaten during Hanukkah. Latkes are said to represent the oil that miraculously lasted for eight days.

Hanukkah is a time for giving gifts, playing dreidels, and spending time with family and friends. Dreidels are four-sided spinning tops that are played during Hanukkah. Each side of the dreidel has a Hebrew letter on it that stands for Nes Gadol Hayah Sham, which means "A great miracle happened there." Dreidels are a popular game for children to play during Hanukkah.

Hanukkah's dreidel game isn't just about spinning a top with Hebrew letters. Historically, it was a way to study the Torah in secret during times when it was forbidden.

kwanzaa 🖤

Kwanzaa is a week-long celebration from December 26th to January 1st each year. Kwanzaa was created in 1966 by Dr. Maulana Karenga to celebrate African heritage, unity, and community building. The name Kwanzaa comes from the Swahili phrase "matunda ya kwanza," which means "first fruits." Kwanzaa is a vibrant and meaningful holiday celebrated by African Americans and people of African descent.

Seven Days and Seven Principles: Kwanzaa lasts for seven days and centers around seven guiding principles, known as Nguzo Saba, which emphasize the values unity, self-determination, collective work and responsibility, cooperative economics, purpose, creativity, and faith. Each day of Kwanzaa focuses on one principle.

Symbols and Decorations: Kwanzaa is marked by rich symbols, including the Kinara (candle holder), seven candles (Mishumaa Saba), mazao (crops), vibunzi (ears of corn), the kikombe cha umoja (unity cup), and zawadi (gifts). These symbols represent ancestral traditions and aspirations for the future.

Happy Kwanzaa greeting card image with seven candles in traditional African colors - red, black, and green. Photo by Caelestiss via depositphotos.com

Lighting the Candles: The Kwanzaa Kinara holds seven candles. Similar to the Menorah in Hanukkah, each night, a candle is lit, starting with the black candle placed in the center, which represents unity. The remaining candles are red (self-determination), green (collective work and responsibility), and black (faith).

Feast of Karamu: On December 31st, the Kwanzaa feast known as Karamu takes place. Families and friends gather to share traditional African dishes, engage in cultural performances, and express gratitude for the year's blessings.

Non-Religious Celebration: Kwanzaa is a non-religious holiday that provides African Americans and people of African descent with an opportunity to celebrate their culture and history in a way that's inclusive of diverse beliefs and backgrounds.

Creative Expression: Artistic expression, including music, poetry, and visual arts, is an integral part of Kwanzaa celebrations. People create and share their work as a means of embracing creativity and preserving cultural heritage.

three kings' day

Three Kings' Day, also known as Epiphany or Dia de los Reyes, is celebrated by various cultures around the world, particularly in Latin American and Spanish-speaking countries such as Puerto Rico, Mexico, Spain, and the Dominican Republic.

This Christian holiday celebrates the arrival of the Three Kings (or Wise Men) to visit the baby Jesus.

Date and Significance: Three Kings' Day is celebrated on January 6th, 12 days after Christmas. It marks the arrival of the three Wise Men or Magi (Melchior, Caspar, and Balthazar) who brought gifts to the baby Jesus. This event is considered the manifestation of Christ to the Gentiles, symbolizing the revelation of Jesus as the Son of God.

Gift-Giving Tradition: Similar to the way gifts are exchanged on Christmas, Three Kings' Day is also associated with gift-giving. In some cultures, children leave their shoes out on the night of January 5th, and on the morning of January 6th, they find gifts, sweets, and sometimes money left by the Three Kings.

Rosca de Reyes or Three Kings' Cake. Photo by agcuesta1 via depositphotos.com

Rosca de Reyes: One of the most iconic traditions of Three Kings' Day is the consumption of Rosca de Reyes. This ring-shaped sweet bread is decorated with candied fruits to resemble jewels, and sometimes a figurine of Baby Jesus is hidden inside. The person who finds the figurine in their slice is traditionally responsible for hosting a feast on Candlemas (Dia de la Candelaria) on February 2nd.

Parades and Festivities: Many countries celebrate Three Kings' Day with lively parades and festive processions. People dress up as the Three Wise Men and travel through the streets, tossing sweets and small gifts to the crowds. These parades often feature vibrant costumes, music, and dancing.

Religious Services: In addition to the festive customs, religious services are an integral part of Three Kings' Day celebrations. Churches hold special masses and ceremonies to commemorate the arrival of the Magi and to reflect on the spiritual significance of the event.

diwali 🪔

Diwali is a Hindu festival of light celebrated across India and by Indian communities worldwide, making it one of the most widely observed festivals in the world. It's also celebrated

The Date of Diwali: The festival's date varies each year, as it's determined by the lunar calendar. It usually falls between October and November. The Diwali festival also signifies the start of a new financial year for many businesses in India, with accounts being settled and new books opened on this auspicious day.

Diwali diya lamps. Photo by akhilesh via depositphotos.com

Inviting Prosperity and Happiness: Diwali involves cleaning and decorating homes with colorful rangoli designs and lighting oil lamps called diyas to invite prosperity and happiness.

Sweets, Treats, and Feasts: Families exchange gifts, share sweets, and engage in feasting during Diwali to honor the victory of light over darkness.

Diwali Fireworks: Fireworks are a major part of Diwali celebrations, symbolizing the triumphant return of Lord Rama to his kingdom after defeating the demon king Ravana. While fireworks are a major part of Diwali celebrations, the festival actually originated as a harvest festival, with the lighting of lamps symbolizing the triumph of light over darkness.

dongzhi festival

Dongzhi Festival is a major holiday in Chinese culture. Dongzhi is typically celebrated around December 21st or 22nd, coinciding with the shortest day and longest night of the year. Dongzhi is also known as "Winter Arrives" in Chinese, reflecting the seasonal transition. It's a time to welcome the arrival of winter and focus on nourishing the body with warm foods and tonics.

Dumplings and Rice Balls: Some families in China celebrate Dongzhi with a custom called "chishi," which involves making and eating dumplings together to ward off the cold and promote good fortune. Tang yuan—glutinous rice balls often filled with sesame, peanuts, or sweet bean paste—are a traditional food enjoyed during Dongzhi. Families gather during Dongzhi to eat tang yuan, symbolizing family unity and togetherness.

Tang yuan dumplings for Dongzhi. Photo by spukkato via depositphotos.com

Symbol of Yin and Yang: Dongzhi Festival represents the balance of Yin and Yang in Chinese philosophy. As the longest night of the year, it symbolizes the peak of Yin (darkness), while the subsequent days gradually increase Yang (light) as daylight hours become longer.

Cultural Diversity: While Dongzhi is widely celebrated in China, it's also observed in other East Asian countries like Taiwan, Vietnam, and parts of Korea and Japan. Each region may have its own unique customs and variations of the festival.

saint lucia's day 🇸🇪

Saint Lucia's Day is widely celebrated in Scandinavian countries, particularly in Sweden, on December 13th. The holiday is associated with light and warmth during the dark winter months, and young girls dress as Saint Lucia in white robes with a crown of candles on their heads.

Saint Lucia's Day marks the beginning of the Christmas season in Sweden and embodies the spirit of bringing light to darkness.

Little girl dressed as St. Lucia with the white robe and crown of lingonberry branches and candles. Photo by elena.degano via depositphotos.com

Honoring St. Lucy: St. Lucia's Day is dedicated to Saint Lucy, a young Christian martyr from Sicily. Legend has it that she brought food and light to persecuted Christians hiding in the catacombs, wearing a wreath of candles on her head to keep her hands free.

Symbol of Light: The central theme of St. Lucia's Day is light during the darkest time of the year. It signifies hope, the triumph of light over darkness, and the return of longer days after the winter solstice.

Wearing the Crown: One of the most distinctive traditions involves a young girl chosen to portray St. Lucia. She wears a white robe symbolizing purity, and a wreath or crown of lingonberry branches adorned with real candles. The crown represents the burning halo of St. Lucy.

Early Morning Celebration: St. Lucia's Day is celebrated early in the morning, before sunrise. The St. Lucia figure leads a procession, often accompanied by girls dressed in white gowns, singing traditional songs and carrying candles.

Saffron Buns and Breakfast: Saffron buns, known as "Lussekatter" or "Lucia buns," are a delicious treat associated with this holiday. These sweet, saffron-flavored pastries are often served as part of a special St. Lucia's Day breakfast.

St. Lucia's Role: In many Scandinavian countries, a local girl is chosen to portray St. Lucia in processions, parades, and ceremonies. The chosen girl wears a white gown, a red sash, and the iconic crown of candles.

Family Celebrations: Families come together to celebrate St. Lucia's Day by enjoying breakfast with saffron buns, gingerbread cookies, and mulled wine. The eldest daughter often plays the role of St. Lucia in family celebrations.

Festive Processions: Throughout Scandinavia, schools, churches, and communities organize processions to mark St. Lucia's Day. Participants dress in white and sing songs while carrying candles or lanterns, creating a beautiful display of light.

Winter Festivities: St. Lucia's Day serves as an important prelude to Christmas festivities in Scandinavian countries. It sets a cheerful tone and reminds people of the importance of spreading light and kindness during the holiday season.

Cultural Diversity: While St. Lucia's Day is most commonly associated with Sweden, it is also celebrated in Norway, Denmark, Finland, and in Scandinavian communities around the world.

boxing day

Boxing Day, celebrated on December 26th, has a delightful array of traditions, surprises, and origins that vary across the globe. While it's not celebrated everywhere, the countries that do observe it have their own unique spin on this day of post-Christmas revelry.

Medieval Origins: The origins of Boxing Day are traced back to medieval England when wealthy households would give "Christmas boxes" filled with gifts, money, and leftovers to their servants as a token of appreciation.

Official Holiday: Boxing Day is an official holiday in several countries, including the United Kingdom, Canada, Australia, New Zealand, South Africa, and some other Commonwealth nations.

Modern Day Boxing Day Traditions: Sporty Start: In the UK, Boxing Day is synonymous with sports. Football (soccer) matches and horse races are popular events that draw massive crowds to stadiums.

Sales Spectacle: In many countries, including the UK, Canada, and Australia, Boxing Day marks the start of major sales and discounts.

Outdoor Activities: In Australia, it's a time for outdoor activities like picnics, beach trips, and enjoying the summer weather.

Giving Back: Some places focus on charitable activities, reflecting the spirit of giving. People donate to various causes, shelters, and food banks.

Charity Challenges: In the UK, "Boxing Day Dips" involve brave souls taking a chilly dip in the sea to raise money for charity.

Bubble and Squeak: Leftovers from the big Christmas feast become the star of the show on Boxing Day. One famous dish that comes from these leftovers is called Bubble and Squeak. This tradition began in the UK during the 19th century as a clever way to use up the extra vegetables from the Christmas meal. The quirky name "Bubble and Squeak" refers to the sounds the veggies make while they're cooking in the pan.

Traditional bubble and squeak made from Christmas dinner leftovers. Photo by the author.

So, what's in Bubble and Squeak? Well, it's mainly made from the veggies that were cooked the day before, like the roasted or boiled potatoes and Brussels sprouts. You can also add in other leftover veggies if you want. All these ingredients get cooked together in a pan, creating a dish with a mix of crispy and soft textures that's really tasty! Often served with chutney.

12
famous christmas stories

E xplore the enchanting world of timeless tales that capture the essence of Christmas spirit. In this chapter, we'll journey through the pages of classic and beloved stories that have warmed hearts for generations. From Dickens' 'A Christmas Carol' to Dr. Seuss' 'How the Grinch Stole Christmas!' and beyond, these narratives continue to kindle the magic of the holiday season. Join us as we delve into the enduring power of these famous Christmas stories.

"a christmas carol" by charles dickens (1843)

This novella tells the story of Ebenezer Scrooge, a miserly old man, who is visited by the ghosts of Christmas Past, Present, and Future. Through their guidance, Scrooge undergoes a transformative journey, learning the importance of kindness, generosity, and the true spirit of Christmas.

Dickens wrote "A Christmas Carol" in just six weeks to address the harsh social realities of his time. The novella played a role in popularizing Christmas traditions like feasting, caroling, and charitable giving. It introduced iconic phrases like "Bah, humbug!" and contributed to the revival of Christmas as a joyful holiday.

"the gift of the magi" by o. henry (1905)

This short story follows a young couple, Jim and Della, who are struggling financially but want to give each other meaningful Christmas gifts. Their love is beautifully captured in their self-less acts during the Christmas season. The story is a touching reminder of the profound meaning of giving and sacrifice.

"The Gift of the Magi" is famous for its surprise twist ending, showcasing the power of sacrifice and unconditional love. The story's title references the biblical magi who brought gifts to the infant Jesus, emphasizing the parallels between selflessness and the true spirit of Christmas.

"the polar express" by chris van allsburg (1985)

In this enchanting picture book, a young boy boards a magical train to the North Pole on Christmas Eve. He embarks on a journey filled with wonder, friendship, and the belief in the spirit of Christmas. The story celebrates the importance of faith, imagination, and the joy of believing.

The train's number "1225" holds special significance. It refers to December 25, Christmas Day, adding an extra layer of magic to the story's setting. The Pere Marquette 1225 locomotive, which serves as the inspiration for the story's train, is a real steam locomotive located in Michigan. It's often called the "North Pole Express" during the holiday season and offers rides to families.

— Did Yule Know?!

"how the grinch stole christmas!" by dr. seuss (1957)

In this whimsical story, the Grinch plots to steal Christmas from the cheerful Whos of Whoville by taking their presents, decorations, and feast. However, he learns that the holiday spirit cannot be stolen and discovers the true meaning of Christmas through the kindness of the Whos.

Dr. Seuss wrote "How the Grinch Stole Christmas!" as a response to concerns about commercialization overshadowing the holiday's significance. The story emphasizes the idea that Christmas is about more than material possessions—it's about love, togetherness, and generosity.

"the night before christmas" by clement clarke moore (1823)

Also known as "A Visit from St. Nicholas," this poem depicts a whimsical visit from Santa Claus on Christmas Eve. It introduces iconic imagery of Santa, his sleigh, and his reindeer, as well as familiar lines like "'Twas the night before Christmas."

This poem was first published anonymously in the Troy Sentinel newspaper on December 23, 1823. The poem quickly gained popularity and became one of the most famous and enduring Christmas poems in the English language. It helped establish the modern image of Santa Claus and popularized the names of his reindeer, including Rudolph.

While Moore is often credited with creating the story, some debate exists about its true authorship.

"the nutcracker and the mouse king" by e.t.a. hoffmann (1816)

This fairy tale follows a young girl named Marie who receives a nutcracker doll as a Christmas gift. The doll comes to life, and Marie embarks on a magical journey to a realm of fantastical creatures and battles between the Nutcracker Prince and the Mouse King.

"The Nutcracker and the Mouse King" served as the basis for Pyotr Ilyich Tchaikovsky's famous ballet, "The Nutcracker." The story's enchanting elements have captivated audiences for generations, making it a staple of holiday performances.

13
famous christmas movies & television specials

These timeless movies and television specials have become integral parts of the holiday season, bringing joy, laughter, and heartwarming messages to families around the world. Whether it's learning that "the best way to spread Christmas cheer is singing loud for all to hear" or embracing the power of kindness and redemption, these films have a special place in our hearts and remind us of the magic that surrounds us during this festive time of year.

dr. seuss' how the grinch stole christmas

Animated Television Special (1966): This animated television special follows the story of the Grinch, a bitter creature who despises Christmas and attempts to steal all the holiday joy from the Whos of Whoville by taking their presents, decorations, and even the food for their feast. However, the Whos' spirit of togetherness and love teaches the Grinch the true meaning of Christmas.

Fun Fact: The special features the iconic voice narration of Boris Karloff, who also provides the voice for the Grinch. The story's catchy song "You're a Mean One, Mr. Grinch" was composed by Albert Hague, with lyrics by Dr. Seuss himself.

Live-Action Film (2000): This live-action film stars Jim Carrey as the Grinch and explores the backstory of the Grinch's transformation from a young outcast to a holiday-hating recluse. The film maintains the core message of the original story, focusing on the power of love, kindness, and the spirit of Christmas to change hearts.

Fun Fact: Jim Carrey, who played the Grinch, had to undergo extensive makeup and prosthetics to transform into the character. The process took several hours each day, and Carrey described it as being like "being buried alive."

a charlie brown christmas (1965)

This animated television special is a beloved holiday classic. The story follows the iconic Peanuts characters, led by the lovable Charlie Brown, as they navigate the challenges and joys of the Christmas season. Charlie Brown struggles with the commercialization of Christmas and sets out on a journey to find the true meaning of the holiday.

Originally, the special was rejected by several television networks because they thought it was too depressing. Thankfully it did finally air and has won three Emmy Awards. It's been translated into over 20 languages and has been broadcast in over 100 countries. It's often ranked among the best Christmas television specials ever made.

Fun Fact: The voices of the characters are provided by real children, giving the special an authentic and endearing quality.

it's a wonderful life (1946)

In 1946, *It's a Wonderful Life* took audiences on a journey with George Bailey, a man who learns the impact he has made on his small town through a guardian angel. It was initially a box office disappointment, but gained popularity and critical acclaim through repeated television broadcasts in the 1980s. It has since become a timeless classic and a beloved Christmas film, often ranked as one of the greatest films of all time.

Fun Fact: The film's snow scenes were created using a mixture of foamite, sugar, and water, which proved challenging for the actors due to its stickiness.

a christmas carol (1951)

The most famous version of the *A Christmas Carol* movie is often considered to be the 1951 film titled *Scrooge* in the UK and *A Christmas Carol* in the USA. This version stars Alastair Sim as Ebenezer Scrooge and is renowned for its faithful adaptation of Charles Dickens' classic story and Sim's memorable performance.

Fun Fact: Alastair Sim, who played Scrooge, often stayed in character even when the cameras weren't rolling, leading the crew to refer to him as "the man who hated Christmas."

There have been well over 50 film and television adaptations of *A Christmas Carol*, each offering its own unique take on the classic tale of Ebenezer Scrooge's transformation.

miracle on 34th street (1947)

Released in 1947, *Miracle on 34th Street* follows the heartwarming story of a man who claims to be the real Santa Claus, leading to a courtroom trial to prove his authenticity.

Fun Fact: The film's outdoor scenes were actually shot during Macy's Thanksgiving Day Parade, and the enthusiastic reactions of the crowd were genuine as they had no idea a film was being made.

home alone (1990)

Home Alone, released in 1990, became an instant holiday classic, as young Kevin McCallister must defend his home from burglars after being accidentally left behind during Christmas vacation.

Fun Fact: The iconic scream that Marv (played by Daniel Stern) lets out after the tarantula falls on his face was real.

elf (2003)

Elf, from 2003, tells the hilarious story of Buddy, a human who was raised at the North Pole by elves, as he embarks on a journey to find his real father in New York City.

Fun Fact: The burp that Buddy lets out after drinking a two-liter bottle of soda was recorded by notable voice actor,

Maurice LaMarche, maybe best known as Brain from *Pinky and the Brain!*

the polar express (2004)

In 2004, *The Polar Express* whisked audiences away on a magical train ride to the North Pole, following a young boy's adventure to rediscover the joy of believing in Santa Claus.

Fun Fact: Tom Hanks provided the voices for multiple characters in the film, including the conductor, the boy, the father, and Santa Claus.

love actually (2003)

Love Actually, released in 2003, weaves together interconnected love stories during the holiday season in London, capturing the warmth and complexity of human relationships.

Fun Fact: The film features a real-life wedding proposal that was staged at the airport during the arrival scene, and the woman's genuine surprise is captured on camera.

national lampoon's christmas vacation (1989)

In 1989, *National Lampoon's Christmas Vacation* hilariously depicted the Griswold family's attempts at having a perfect Christmas, leading to a series of comical mishaps.

Fun Fact: The character of Uncle Lewis (played by William Hickey) was scripted to have a flaming toupee in one scene, but the special effects went awry and resulted in actual flames.

a christmas story (1983)

Set in the 1940s, *A Christmas Story* chronicles young Ralphie's quest to convince his parents, his teacher, and even Santa that a Red Ryder BB gun is the perfect Christmas gift.

Fun Fact: The film's iconic leg lamp was based on a real lampshade called the "Classic Full Size Leg Lamp," that author Jean Shepherd saw in a store window. The lamp became so popular after the release of the movie that it is now sold as a merchandise item and a replica of it can be found at the Christmas Story House and Museum in Cleveland, Ohio.

the santa clause (1994)

In *The Santa Clause*, released in 1994, Tim Allen's character suddenly becomes Santa Claus after inadvertently causing the previous Santa to fall off his roof.

Fun Fact: The film's snow is made of a biodegradable material used in baby diapers, ensuring it was safe for the environment.

scrooged (1988)

Scrooged provides a modern twist on "A Christmas Carol," following Bill Murray's character, a cynical TV executive, as he's visited by ghosts and shown the error of his ways.

Fun Fact: The film's live audience reactions during the TV broadcast scenes were real, as the scenes were filmed in front of an actual audience.

die hard (1988)

Die Hard isn't your typical Christmas film, yet its action-packed story set during a Christmas party has helped it become a holiday classic for many. There is a debate about whether this film should even count as a Christmas movie. It's often referred to as an "action movie set during Christmas." Despite the debate, it has become a popular choice for some as a non-traditional Christmas film, and is often included in holiday movie marathons.

Fun Fact: The film's Nakatomi Plaza was actually the headquarters of 20th Century Fox, and the company had to rent out several of its own floors for the film's production.

white christmas (1954)

In *White Christmas*, two entertainers team up to save a failing Vermont inn, and their efforts lead to a heartwarming holiday performance.

Fun Fact: The song "White Christmas" originally appeared in the 1942 film *Holiday Inn*, also starring Bing Crosby.

the nightmare before christmas (1993)

Combining Halloween and Christmas, *The Nightmare Before Christmas* follows Jack Skellington's attempt to bring Christmas to Halloween Town with whimsically eerie results.

Fun Fact: The film was entirely stop-motion animated and took three years to complete.

What's The Most Popular Christmas Movie Of All Time?

The answer to the most popular Christmas movie of all time can vary depending on different factors such as personal preferences, region, and cultural influences. However, one movie that consistently ranks among the top and is often considered a timeless classic is It's a Wonderful Life *(1946).*

— Did Yule Know?!

hallmark christmas movies

Hallmark Christmas movies are a popular genre of television movies typically released during the holiday season. The movies usually feature heartwarming stories about love, family, and friendship, set against the backdrop of a snowy Christmas town. Hallmark Christmas movies often follow a predictable formula, but they continue to be popular with viewers who appreciate their feel-good messages and happy endings.

The Movie that Started it All: The Hallmark Channel Christmas movie tradition started with broadcast television network ABC. In 1989, ABC aired the first made-for-TV Christmas movie, *The Christmas Wife*. The movie was a huge hit, and it inspired other networks to start producing their own Christmas movies.

Familiar Filming Locations: Many Hallmark Christmas movies are shot in picturesque small towns in Canada. The charming backdrops and snow-covered landscapes contribute to the cozy and festive atmosphere. An added bonus is Canada offers tax incentives for filmmakers who shoot in the country.

Fast Filming: Each Hallmark Channel Christmas movie only takes a couple of weeks to film. This is because the movies follow a very predictable formula, which makes them easy to produce quickly. The formula typically includes a meet-cute between two people who are opposites in some way, a small-town setting, a family heirloom that plays a role in the story, and a Christmas miracle.

The Most-Watched Hallmark Christmas Movie: The most-watched Hallmark Channel Christmas movie of all time is Christmas Under Wraps, which aired in 2014. Over 5.8 million people watched its premiere.

Most-Popular Hallmark Christmas Movie Actress: Candace Cameron Bure is the most popular actress in Hallmark Channel Christmas movies. She has starred in over 20 Christmas movies for the network.

Watched Worldwide: Hallmark Channel Christmas movies are watched by viewers all over the world.

christmas in july 😎

Hallmark Channel's "Christmas in July" programming is a mid-year treat for fans who can't get enough of holiday cheer. It's a chance to enjoy some of their favorite Christmas movies during the summer months.

14

jobs that only happen at christmastime

The holiday season brings about a variety of unique and festive jobs that pop up just in time to spread Christmas cheer. Here are some fun and unusual seasonal jobs and interesting facts about each:

mall santas 🎅

Perhaps the most iconic seasonal job, Mall Santas are tasked with bringing joy to children by listening to their wish lists and posing for photos. These jolly individuals undergo training to embody the spirit of Santa Claus and often have a knack for making holiday dreams come true.

christmas tree decorator 🧑‍🎨

Christmas tree decorators are the creative wizards who take ordinary trees and transform them into enchanting holiday centerpieces. With an eye for design and an artistic touch, these skilled professionals curate themes, select ornaments, and meticulously arrange lights to craft stunning and harmonious displays. Whether working independently or as part of a business, their ability to balance, place lights, and select ornaments results in personalized and captivating designs.

christmas tree lot attendant

These individuals help customers select the perfect Christmas tree, trim the bottom for freshness, and even tie the tree securely to their vehicles. It's a job that requires knowledge of different tree varieties and excellent customer service skills.

gift wrapper

Gift wrapping is an art in itself, and during the holiday season, skilled gift wrappers work in stores to expertly wrap presents with intricate designs and bows, making gifts look even more appealing.

ice sculptors

In colder regions, ice sculptors craft intricate sculptures from blocks of ice, turning ordinary spaces into winter wonderlands. These ephemeral artworks often grace festivals, events, and displays. While ice sculptors can work outside of the Christmas season, they are often their busiest during the holiday season.

christmas light installer

Christmas light installers hang Christmas lights on homes, businesses, and other buildings. They also repair and replace lights that are damaged or burned out.

christmas lightshow choreographers

In recent years, synchronized Christmas light displays have become popular. Choreographers use technology to program intricate light shows that dance to the rhythm of holiday tunes, creating stunning visual spectacles.

15

outside of holiday festivities, december is a busy month

Beyond the twinkling lights, festive gatherings, and holiday cheer, December is a month of hidden stories and surprising statistics. While the world celebrates the season of giving, it's also a time for significant life events, travel adventures, and unique challenges. In this chapter, we delve into the lesser-known aspects of December, unveiling the month's vibrant tapestry of experiences that go beyond the traditional festivities. From marriage proposals to job searches, discover the intriguing tales that unfold in the midst of this joyful season.

marriage proposals

December is a popular month for marriage proposals, as many couples choose to celebrate their love during the festive season. According to Bridebook, a popular wedding planning app, more than 100,000 engagements occur during the Christmas season, with 40% taking place between Christmas Eve and New Year's Day.

United States: According to The Wedding Report's Complete Wedding Market Report for the United States, 15.5% of all engagements take place within the final month of the year (for context, no other month surpasses 9%!).

United Kingdom: According to a study by YouGov, a British market research company, 16% of all proposals in the UK happen during the Christmas season.

Canada: A study by WeddingWire, a wedding planning website, found that 14% of all proposals in Canada happen during the Christmas season.

Australia: According to a study by Brides, an Australian wedding planning magazine, 12% of all proposals in Australia happen during the Christmas season.

Germany: A study by Statista, a German statistics portal, found that 10% of all proposals in Germany happen during the Christmas season.

There are a few reasons why the Christmas season is such a popular time for marriage proposals. First, it is a time of year when people are feeling happy and festive, which can create a romantic atmosphere. Second, many people are surrounded by their loved ones during the holidays, which can make it a special occasion to propose. Third, Christmas is a time when people are thinking about the future, which can make it a natural time to consider marriage.

december weddings

While, there are high numbers of marriage proposals happening in December, that doesn't mean there are a high number of marriages. The number of weddings that actually take place during the Christmas season is much smaller. According to the National Center for Health Statistics, only 11% of marriages in the United States happen in December.

december: the month of beginnings!

Did you know that September is the most popular birth month? It turns out that all those cozy holiday celebrations and winter wonderland vibes in December can lead to a higher rate of conceptions. With September being the top month for birthdays, it's safe to say that December is a month of beginnings in more ways than one!

increased travel

The Christmas season is the busiest travel time of year in the United States. In 2021, an estimated 109 million people traveled by car, plane, or train during the holiday season. After Thanksgiving, Christmas is the second busiest travel period of the year in the United States

The most popular Christmas travel destinations in the United States are Orlando, Florida; Las Vegas, Nevada; and New York City.

The most popular Christmas travel destinations internationally are London, England; Paris, France; and Rome, Italy.

increased shopping

Christmas shopping is a big part of the holiday season. In 2022, the average American spent $1,000 on Christmas shopping, and online shopping accounted for 54% of all Christmas shopping. Electronics, clothing, and gift cards were the most popular Christmas gifts, and Black Friday, Cyber Monday, and Christmas Eve are the most popular Christmas shopping days.

a few additional pounds ⚖️

While there's no one-size-fits-all answer, studies suggest that people may gain around 1 to 2 pounds (0.45 to 0.9 kilograms) on average during the holiday season, which typically spans from Thanksgiving to New Year's Day. However, it's important to note that these numbers can vary widely from person to person.

increased (and unique!) injuries 😷

Tis the season to be jolly, but it's also the season to be careful! Every year, thousands of people and pets are injured in Christmas-related accidents. Here are just a few to be aware of:

Falls are the most common Christmas injury. Accounting for over 40% of all Christmas-related ER visits, falls are the most common injury during the Christmas season. Falls can happen while decorating your Christmas tree, putting up lights, sledding or shoveling snow.

Christmas lights can be dangerous. In addition to falls, Christmas lights can also cause electrical shocks, burns, and eye injuries. Be sure to use lights that are UL-listed (tested and certified to be safe) and to never leave them on unattended.

Chestnuts can be hot. Roasting chestnuts over an open fire is a classic Christmas tradition, but it's important to be careful not to burn yourself. Use a roasting pan with a lid to protect your hands and face from the heat.

Burns from candles. Candles are a popular Christmas decoration, but they can also be dangerous. Be sure to keep candles away from children and pets, and never leave them burning unattended.

Don't drink and drive. Alcohol consumption is on the rise during the Christmas season, and it's important to remember that drinking and driving is never a good idea. If you're going to be drinking, have a designated driver or call a cab.

Be careful with sharp objects. Many Christmas activities, especially gift wrapping, involve the use of sharp objects such as knives, scissors, and needles. Be sure to use caution when handling these items to avoid cuts and injuries.

Injuries during holiday parties. Holiday parties are a common setting for Christmas-related injuries. In 2022, over 30% of all Christmas-related ER visits happened during a holiday party.

Injuries among family pets. Ingestion of Christmas decorations is the most common pet Christmas-related injury, accounting for over 40% of all pet Christmas-related ER visits. Pets may ingest Christmas decorations such as tinsel, ornaments, and lights, which can cause choking, intestinal blockages, or poisoning.

increased job searches 🤨

Many people take advantage of the holiday season to reassess their career goals and seek new job opportunities. Online job searches and applications tend to spike during December as individuals make resolutions for the upcoming year.

16
fun modern christmas traditions

Step into the world of twinkling lights, cozy gatherings, and joyful festivities as we dive into the enchanting realm of modern Christmas traditions! While cherished customs like decorating trees and hanging stockings have deep roots, there's a whole sleigh-load of delightful and playful traditions that have sprung up in recent times.

From donning outrageously festive sweaters to cozying up in matching Christmas pajamas, this chapter unveils the merry and quirky traditions that have become an integral part of the holiday season.

ugly christmas sweaters 🧶

The Ugly Christmas Sweater phenomenon isn't just about staying warm—it's a merry mashup of holiday spirit and quirky fashion! Originating in the 1980s, these garishly delightful sweaters were once a fashion faux pas but have now become a beloved holiday tradition. As the winter winds blow, people across the globe proudly don their most outlandish and over-the-top sweaters to embrace the playful side of the season.

Origins of Ugly Christmas Sweaters: The Ugly Christmas Sweater trend began as a tongue-in-cheek reaction to the traditionally stylish holiday outfits. What started as a small gathering in Vancouver, Canada, where friends showed off their quirkiest sweaters, has now become a worldwide phenomenon. Who knew that embracing the gaudy and extravagant could bring so much joy?

Why the Ugly Factor? It's all about spreading laughter and warmth during the holiday season. The concept of wearing something intentionally "ugly" is a lighthearted way to connect and bond with others, embracing the spirit of togetherness and camaraderie that defines the season.

Funky Favorites: The Ugly Christmas Sweater universe is brimming with creativity. From sweaters adorned with 3D reindeer noses to ones that light up with LED lights, the range of designs is as vast as the distance to the North Pole itself. It's a chance to showcase your individual style while celebrating the holiday spirit in the funkiest way possible.

Ugly Christmas Sweater Day: There is an official Ugly Christmas Sweater Day celebrated on the third Friday of December each year. People don their most outrageous and tacky sweaters to embrace the festive spirit.

Create-Your-Own Ugly Christmas Sweater: Many people prefer to create their own ugly Christmas sweaters by adding peculiar decorations like pom-poms, garlands, felt appliques, or even battery-operated lights. Thrift stores are also popular destinations for finding authentic vintage and kitschy sweaters.

Ugly Christmas Sweater Fun Run: Some cities organize fun runs or races where participants wear their most outrageous Christmas sweaters while running or walking. These events combine fitness and festive spirit in a lighthearted way.

Ugly Christmas Rash Guard - photo rendering by Midjourney

🇦🇺 Ugly Christmas Rash Guards in Australia

While Australians might be celebrating Christmas in the heat of summer, they've put their unique twist on the Ugly Christmas Sweater trend. Instead of heavy woolen sweaters, Australians have embraced the concept of Ugly Christmas

Rash Guards. These are long-sleeved, lightweight, and UV-protective shirts worn during beach activities to shield the skin from the sun. These festive and often hilarious rash guards feature themes like Santa riding a surfboard, or kangaroos wearing Santa hats. They combine holiday cheer with coastal vibes.

New Zealand's Ugly Christmas T-shirts

In New Zealand, there is a playful alternative to ugly Christmas sweaters known as "Ugly Christmas T-shirts." With Christmas falling during their summer season, people opt for lightweight and short-sleeved shirts with humorous and eye-catching Christmas-themed designs.

Sweden's "Jultröja"

Sweden has its own version of ugly Christmas sweaters called "Jultröja" or "Yule Sweaters." These sweaters typically feature bright colors, kitschy patterns, and sometimes even built-in electronic lights or sound effects.

Finland's Tacky Christmas Jumper's

In Finland, there is a tradition called "Tacky Christmas Jumper Day" where people wear gaudy and over-the-top sweaters to embrace the festive spirit. It is often accompanied by fundraising events for charity.

christmas pajamas

Wearing matching or festive Christmas pajamas has become a cherished holiday tradition for many families. People of all ages don whimsical sleepwear to celebrate the holiday season. It's a cozy way to create a sense of togetherness and unity while opening presents, enjoying breakfast, or simply lounging by the

Christmas tree.

The tradition of Christmas pajamas has gained popularity in recent years due to the availability of matching sets for the whole family, creating fun photo opportunities.

secret santa & elephant exchanges 🐘

Secret Santa exchanges and White Elephant gifts are both popular and fun gift-giving traditions that add an element of surprise and entertainment to holiday celebrations.

Secret Santa Exchanges: Secret Santa is a gift exchange where participants draw names randomly to determine who they will be buying a gift for. The twist is that the identity of the gift giver remains a secret until the gifts are exchanged. This adds an element of mystery and excitement as participants try to guess who their Secret Santa might be. Secret Santa exchanges can take place within families, among friends, in workplaces, and even in online communities.

White Elephant Gifts: White Elephant gift exchanges, also known as Yankee Swaps or Dirty Santas, are games that involves participants bringing wrapped gifts, and then taking turns selecting a gift from the pool, or "stealing" a gift that someone else has already chosen. This tradition adds an element of competitiveness and laughter, as participants try to end up with the most entertaining or sought-after gift.

White Elephant gifts often have a fun and playful twist, with participants getting creative by bringing items that are unexpected, humorous, or even mildly outrageous. It's a lighthearted way to exchange gifts while fostering a sense of camaraderie and shared amusement among participants.

Both Secret Santa exchanges and White Elephant gifts have become beloved holiday traditions that encourage laughter, interaction, and the joy of giving and receiving thoughtful (or delightfully unconventional) presents.

Why White Elephant? In times gone by, it's said that the King of Siam had a unique way of punishing someone: by gifting them a white elephant. This sacred animal, while majestic, was a financial burden and near-impossible to keep. This tale paved the way for what we recognize as the White Elephant gift exchanges, where participants bring gifts to swap, steal, or exchange, adding a touch of humor and suspense.

— Did Yule Know?!

holiday photo cards 💚

Sending personalized holiday photo cards to friends and family has become a cherished tradition. People often get creative with themed photoshoots and digital designs to spread holiday cheer.

Fun Fact: The tradition of sending holiday photo cards dates back to the late 19th century. The first photo card is believed to have been sent in the 1890s, featuring a black-and-white image of a family posing for Christmas.

christmas markets & christmas fairs

Christmas market in Frankfurt, Germany. Photo by sborisov via depositphotos.com

Christmas markets are a popular tradition in many European countries, and they are becoming increasingly popular in the United States. The first recorded Christmas market took place in Vienna, Austria in 1298. These markets were originally held to provide supplies for the winter season.

Christmas markets commonly showcase local artisans and their handcrafted goods. They are also known for selling unique Christmas ornaments, and traditional Christmas food and drink. Typical foodstuffs might include gluhwein (mulled wine), bratwurst (grilled sausage) or gingerbread. These markets are a great place to get into the holiday spirit and to do some Christmas shopping.

gingerbread house decorating 🏠

Creating and decorating gingerbread houses has evolved into an art form. People now create intricate and imaginative gingerbread structures, often inspired by famous landmarks, characters, and scenes.

Queen Elizabeth I of England enjoyed decorating gingerbread, and is credited with the idea of decorating gingerbread cookies in the likeness of important guests.

— Did Yule Know?!

---

christmas lights & christmas light tours ✨

Christmas lights. Photo by Hannamariah via depositphotos.com

Elaborate Christmas light displays have become a spectacle during the holiday season, with homes and neighborhoods competing to create the most dazzling and enchanting visual experiences. Some displays are synchronized with music, while others incorporate innovative technology to create jaw-dropping effects.

Fun Fact: Many communities host contests and tours to showcase the best Christmas light displays, contributing to a festive atmosphere and fostering community spirit.

elf on the shelf 🧝

Two elf figurines on a shelf. Photo by erin mckenna on Unsplash

The Elf on the Shelf is a playful holiday tradition that involves an elf figurine who "magically" moves to different locations in the home each night, keeping an eye on children to report back to Santa on their behavior. This tradition has gained traction as parents think up creative and mischievous scenarios for the elf.

Fun Fact: The Elf on the Shelf was inspired by a 2005 children's book written by Carol Aebersold and her daughter Chanda Bell, which tells the story of how Santa's scout elves help him manage his naughty and nice lists. The first Elf on the Shelf was named Fisbee, after a vintage elf that Carol's parents had given her as a child.

christmas movie marathons

Watching a series of favorite Christmas movies has become a beloved tradition for many. Whether it's classic films or modern favorites, cozying up with popcorn and blankets for a movie marathon is a wonderful way to spend the holiday season.

The first-ever Christmas movie marathon was held on December 25, 1972, on WGN-TV in Chicago. The marathon featured 12 Christmas movies, including *It's a Wonderful Life*, *Miracle on 34th Street*, and *A Charlie Brown Christmas*.

The longest Christmas movie marathon ever held was in 2015, on the Hallmark Channel. The marathon featured 24 hours of continuous Christmas movies, including *The Christmas Chronicles*, *The Santa Clause*, and *Home Alone*.

17
guinness world records— christmas related

Get ready to embark on a journey into the magical world of Guinness World Records with a festive twist. From massive gatherings of Santa Clauses to towering Christmas trees, spectacular light displays, and incredible feats, these records capture the spirit of Christmas in all its grandeur. Join us as we explore the most remarkable achievements in the Guinness World Records' Christmas Hall of Fame.

largest gathering of santa clauses 🎅

The record for the largest gathering of people dressed as Santa Claus was achieved in 2014 in Thrissur, Kerala, India on December 27, 2014 with 18, 112 participants. The event was organized to raise money for the needy.

tallest christmas tree 🎄

The world record for the tallest cut Christmas tree is held by a 64.6-meter (212 ft) Douglas fir that was erected and decorated at the Northgate Shopping Center in Seattle, Washington, USA in December 1950.

The tree was cut from Mount Rainier National Park and required a special escort on the highway to the shopping center. It took 125 men to hoist the tree into place. The tree was decorated with 3,600 lights and a star put on top.

most christmas lights on a residential property 🏠

Tim, Grace, Emily, Daniel, and John Gay of LaGrangeville, New York, USA broke their Guinness World Record for the most lights on a residential property in November 2022. They decorated their home with 703,000 lights, linked by over 8 miles (12. 8 km) of extension cord!

Throughout the years, they've had 19 marriage proposals on their property. They often will collaborate with whomever is popping the question by programming the lights to spell out "marry me."

largest christmas cracker 🧨

The largest Christmas cracker ever made measured 207 feet (63.1 meters) in length and 13.6 feet (4.14 meters) in diameter. It was created in Australia in 1991.

tallest snow person ☃

Only a few feet shorter than the Statue of Liberty, snow woman Olympia stood tall at 122 feet, 1 inch tall (37.21 meters) and with a 125-foot diameter at the base. The tallest snow woman record was set in the American state of Maine in February 2008 and about 13 million pounds of snow was used to make her. She wore a 130-foot-long scarf, a 6-foot 6-inch snowflake pendant necklace and had three buttons made from 5-foot truck tires. Her lips were made from car tires, her arms were made using two 30-foot spruce trees and her eyelashes were made using eight pairs of snow skis.

most expensive christmas tree 💰

The most expensive Christmas tree on record was valued at over $11 million and was displayed in the Emirates Palace hotel in Abu Dhabi, UAE, in 2010. The tree was decorated with gold, diamonds, pearls, and other precious stones.

most expensive christmas ornament 💎

The most expensive Christmas ornament ever sold was a Fabergé egg-shaped bauble. It was encrusted with over 3,000 diamonds and sold for £82,000 (approximately $105,000) in 2018.

largest collection of baubles

Sylvia Pope of Swansea, UK, has proudly amassed a remarkable collection of 1,760 Christmas bauble ornaments, securing her a spot in the record books as of December 1, 2021. Notably,

Sylvia's enchanting assortment of baubles takes center stage in her home, where they remain on display throughout the year.

largest snowflake ornament

The largest Christmas snowflake ornament measures 3.196 m (10 ft 5 in) in diameter and was achieved by Universal Studios Japan in Osaka, Japan, on October 28, 2019.

The ornament sits atop Universal Studios Japan's Christmas tree, which has achieved the Guinness World Records title for the most lights on an artificial Christmas tree.

fastest chocolate-eating

While most people savor the chocolates from their advent calendars gradually, enjoying a single treat each day from December 1 to December 24, L.A. Beast took a decidedly different approach. In an astonishing feat, he managed to consume the entire assortment in a mere 1 minute and 27 seconds. This record-breaking feat included the intricate task of opening each door in the correct sequence and consuming the chocolates one by one.

fastest time to eat three mince pies

Mince pies are a beloved household delight during the Christmas season in different parts of the world, yet no one can eat them as fast as Leah Shutkever. Shutkever is a competitive eater and holder of multiple Guinness World Records titles. She secured her place in record-breaking history by accomplishing the fastest time to consume three mince pies—an impressive 52.21 seconds. This remarkable feat took place in London, UK, on September 25, 2019.

largest cup of hot chocolate/cocoa

Setting a new record on December 16, 2017, the title for the Largest Cup of Hot Chocolate/Cocoa belongs to a creation that dwarfs your standard mug by a considerable margin. The impressive feat was accomplished by Soda Springs Mountain Resort in California, USA, which concocted a staggering 4,506.83 liters (1,190.58 US gallons) of this delightful drink.

Photo courtesy of Guinness Book of World Records

For those interested in replicating this colossal concoction, the recipe includes:

- 4,163.95 liters (1,100 US gallons) of water

- 226.79 kg (500 lbs) of hot cocoa mix
- 37.85 liters (10 US gallons) of milk

This gargantuan hot chocolate delight was served at a toasty 41.1 degrees Celsius (106 degrees Fahrenheit).

oldest artificial christmas tree 🎄

Paul Parker from the UK is the proud owner of a cherished artificial Christmas tree that has been a part of his family's history since 1886. Standing at a height of 30 cm (1 ft), the tree is elegantly displayed in an ornate pot. It was initially acquired for his great-great Aunt Lou and is believed to have been purchased from Woolworths. Passed down through generations, the tree was lovingly bequeathed to Paul by his mother, Janet, in 2008, ensuring that the tradition lives on.

largest christmas pudding 🍰

The people of Aughton, Lancashire, UK, came together to create a record-breaking Christmas pudding that tipped the scales at a whopping 3.28 tons (7,231 lb, 10z). This colossal dessert made its grand debut during the Famous Aughton Pudding Festival on July 11, 1992.

largest christmas stocking 🧦

The largest Christmas stocking ever created measured 177 feet and 8.8 inches (54 meters) long and 72 feet and 1.6 inches (22 meters) wide. It was made in Italy in 2011.

largest snowball fight ☃️

The largest snowball fight on record took place in Seattle, Washington, USA, in 2013. A total of 8,200 participants engaged in the epic snowball fight that lasted for 25 minutes.

largest human christmas tree 🧍🧍🧍🧍🧍🧍

The largest human Christmas tree was made up of 4,030 kids and adults of Mission Chengannur in India, on 19 December 2015.The Christmas tree was mostly composed of school children from the village of Chengannur.

Image courtesy or Guinness Book of World Records

most letters to santa collected 📫

The most letters to Santa Claus collected in a single season was 1.6 million letters. This record was achieved by Canada Post in 2016.

most people carolling in one place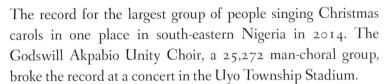

The record for the largest group of people singing Christmas carols in one place in south-eastern Nigeria in 2014. The Godswill Akpabio Unity Choir, a 25,272 man-choral group, broke the record at a concert in the Uyo Township Stadium.

18
sustainable christmas
Eco-friendly Celebrations

In a world that's becoming increasingly conscious of its environmental impact, it's no surprise that the spirit of sustainability has found its way into the realm of Christmas celebrations. From reducing waste to embracing eco-friendly practices, this chapter explores how you can make your holiday season merrier while treading lightly on our planet.

rent a christmas tree 🎄

Did you know that artificial Christmas trees typically need to be used for more than 20 years to have a smaller carbon footprint than buying a fresh tree each year? One way to be more eco-friendly with your Christmas trees is to rent them.

These living Christmas trees are grown in a pot year after year on some Christmas tree farms, can be delivered to a home or company office during the holiday season, and then returned to the Christmas Tree Farm to be taken care of for next year's celebrations.

Fun Fact: Christmas tree rental options extend beyond just the tree itself; some services also provide rental ornaments and decorations to complete the festive look.

reusable wrapping alternatives

Unwrapping presents is a delightful part of Christmas, but it doesn't have to be wasteful. Discover creative ways to wrap gifts using reusable fabric, scarves, or even newspapers. Dive into the art of "furoshiki," the Japanese method of wrapping gifts using cloth, and add an eco-friendly twist to your holiday gifting.

Fun Fact: The Japanese art of furoshiki dates back to the Nara period (710-794 AD), where people used fabric to wrap and transport goods. Nowadays, it's making a comeback as an eco-friendly way to wrap gifts, reducing the need for disposable paper.

led lights shine brightly & efficiently

LED lights have revolutionized Christmas decorating by being energy-efficient and longer-lasting. LED lights can last up to 25,000 hours or more. Not only do they consume up to 80% less energy than traditional incandescent lights, but they also emit less heat, reducing the risk of fire hazards.

Fun Fact: LED lights are so energy-efficient that if every American home replaced just one string of traditional holiday lights with LEDs, it would save enough electricity to power over 200,000 homes for a year.

trash into christmas treasures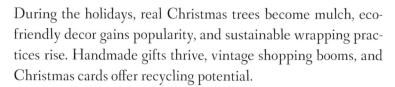

During the holidays, real Christmas trees become mulch, eco-friendly decor gains popularity, and sustainable wrapping practices rise. Handmade gifts thrive, vintage shopping booms, and Christmas cards offer recycling potential.

Repurposing packaging materials, organizing community upcycling workshops, and growing environmental awareness all contribute to sustainable holiday choices, reflecting a collective effort to reduce waste and transform trash into Christmas treasures.

Fun Fact: An estimated 2.5 billion Christmas cards are sold each year in the United States. Encouraging the recycling or repurposing of these cards can help reduce paper waste.

d.i.y. natural wreaths & decorations 🎄

Venture into the world of crafting with nature's finest offerings. Discover how to make beautiful wreaths using pinecones, dried citrus slices, and twigs. These natural creations not only enhance your home's holiday charm but also celebrate the beauty of the outdoors.

Fun Fact: Did you know that making natural wreaths is a time-honored tradition? In ancient Rome, wreaths made from evergreen branches were a symbol of victory, and were worn as crowns during celebrations.

sustainable feasting 🍗

Embrace the farm-to-table philosophy when preparing your Christmas feast. Sourcing local, seasonal ingredients not only supports your community but also reduces the carbon footprint associated with transporting food long distances. Uncover the joy of creating a sustainable holiday meal that's as delicious as it is kind to the Earth.

Fun Fact: According to a study by the Worldwatch Institute, the food miles for the average American meal is around 1,500 miles. Choosing local and seasonal ingredients for your holiday meal can significantly reduce this number and contribute to sustainability.

gifting memories that last

Swap material presents for memorable experiences that leave a lasting impact. Whether it's gifting cooking classes, concert tickets, or a day of outdoor adventures, explore the trend of giving experiences that foster connection and joy, without contributing to clutter.

Fun Fact: Research from the University of Toronto shows that experiences tend to provide longer-lasting happiness compared to material possessions. The memories made from shared experiences can become cherished family stories for years to come.

secondhand surprises: thrifted gifts

Thrifting isn't just about scoring vintage fashion—it's also an eco-friendly way to find unique gifts. Delve into the world of thrifted treasures and discover how pre-loved items can make for heartwarming and sustainable holiday surprises.

Fun Fact: The Japanese concept of "mottainai" promotes the idea of avoiding waste and appreciating the value of items.

Thrifting aligns perfectly with this philosophy, allowing you to find meaningful gifts while reducing waste.

minimalist merry-making

Embrace the minimalist trend by focusing on quality over quantity. Explore the concept of "hygge" and "lagom" as you learn to curate a cozy and balanced holiday ambiance that reduces excess and celebrates the simple joys of the season.

Fun Fact: Hygge is pronounced "hoo-guh" and is a Danish word that doesn't have a direct translation in English. It's often described as a feeling of coziness, contentment, and well-being. Lagom is pronounced "lah-gom" and is a Swedish word. It doesn't have a direct English translation but is often described as "just the right amount" or "balanced."

post-holiday eco-cleanup

The fun doesn't have to end when the holidays do. Uncover creative ways to recycle or repurpose your Christmas decorations once the season is over. From crafting with leftover wrapping paper to donating gently used ornaments, learn how to give your holiday decor a second life.

Fun Fact: Some communities have Christmas tree recycling programs that turn old trees into mulch, which can then be used to enrich soil in local parks and gardens. It's a wonderful way to close the loop on the holiday season.

19

christmas charity and giving back

In the spirit of giving, Christmas is a time when people around the world come together to spread kindness, warmth, and goodwill. From small gestures of generosity to large-scale charitable initiatives, the holiday season fosters a sense of compassion and community that transcends borders. This chapter explores heartwarming stories of Christmas charity, highlighting global acts of kindness that brighten the lives of others during this special time of year.

Christmas isn't just about receiving gifts, it's also a time when people around the world come together to give back to their communities and spread joy to those in need. From volunteering at shelters to donating to charitable causes, the holiday season brings out the best in humanity.

angel trees & gift drives

Many organizations set up "Angel Trees" or "Giving Trees" adorned with paper ornaments that list gift requests from underprivileged children. People choose an ornament, buy the requested gift, and contribute to making a child's Christmas special.

Fun Fact: The tradition of Angel Trees started in the early 1980s and was inspired by the Salvation Army's desire to provide Christmas gifts to children in need.

How to Get Involved: Look for Angel Trees in malls, community centers, and churches. Choose an ornament with a gift request, purchase the item, and help make a child's holiday special.

operation christmas child 📦

Every year, people around the world participate in Operation Christmas Child by packing shoeboxes with toys, school supplies, and hygiene items. These boxes are then distributed to children in need around the world, bringing joy to their faces.

Fun Fact: Operation Christmas Child began in 1990 and has delivered over 178 million gift-filled shoeboxes to children in more than 150 countries.

How to Get Involved: Pack a shoebox with age-appropriate toys, school supplies, and hygiene items. Drop it off at a collection site or build a shoebox online.

random acts of kindness 😊

The "Random Acts of Kindness" phenomenon, where anonymous individuals pay for the purchases of strangers, has become a heartwarming tradition in many places, spreading cheer and surprise during the holiday shopping rush.

Fun Fact: A popular random act of kindness tradition called 'Hanging Coffee' or "suspended coffee" involves individuals purchasing a coffee or meal at a cafe and 'hanging' it for someone in need. When someone less fortunate comes in, they can ask for a 'suspended' item, receiving the pre-purchased coffee or meal, promoting acts of kindness and community support.

How to Get Involved: Surprise someone by covering their coffee, meal, or groceries. Leave a note wishing them a Merry Christmas.

feeding the hungry

Many food banks and soup kitchens see a surge in volunteers and donations during the holiday season, ensuring that those less fortunate can enjoy warm meals and celebrate the spirit of Christmas.

Food banks typically see the highest demand for donations during the winter months, making Christmas a crucial time for support.

Fun Fact: St. Mary's Food Bank in Phoenix, Arizona was the world's first food bank, established in the US in 1967. Since then, many thousands have been set up all over the world, especially in Europe.

How to Get Involved: Donate non-perishable food items to local food banks or volunteer your time to help sort and distribute donations.

operation santa 🔍

Since 1912, United States Postal Service employees and volunteers have answered children's letters to Santa Claus. What started as an initiative to ensure every letter to Santa received a response has grown into a nationwide effort to fulfill the wishes of families in need. Each year, 'Operation Santa' helps thousands of families by granting their holiday wishes for toys, clothing, and other necessities.

Fun Fact: While most children today send letters to Santa at the North Pole, historical letters show creative addresses like "Behind the Moon", Iceland, Ice Street, and Cloudville.

How to Get Involved: To join Operation Santa, contact your local post office for info and eligibility. Pick letters to adopt, shop, and send gifts anonymously. Make the season brighter. Learn more at https://www.uspsoperationsanta.com/

christmas meals for all 👨‍🍳

Communities often organize free or low-cost Christmas dinners for those who might be alone during the holidays or facing financial hardships.

Fun Fact: Some restaurants and community centers offer free Christmas dinners, often staffed by volunteers, to ensure everyone has a warm meal on Christmas Day.

How to Get Involved: Volunteer to serve or help organize a community Christmas dinner. Spread the word to those who might benefit.

donating warmth 🧤

During colder months, "Mitten Trees" and "Scarves of Kindness" initiatives provide warm clothing items for those in need. People hang mittens, scarves, and hats on trees for others to take and stay warm.

Fun Fact: Mitten trees have been a holiday tradition since the 1940s, originally established to provide warm clothing for children in need.

How to Get Involved: Donate new or gently used winter accessories like mittens, hats, and scarves to designated collection points.

santa runs & charity walks 🏃 🏃

Festive fun runs, walks, and swims raise funds for various causes, bringing people together in a lighthearted and charitable way.

Fun Fact: Santa Runs started in the UK in the 1970s and have since become popular in many countries as a festive way to raise funds for charity.

How to Get Involved: Participate in a Santa Run or charity walk in your area. Register, gather pledges, and join the holiday fun while supporting a cause.

hospital visits 🏥

Volunteers dressed as Santa, elves, and other holiday characters visit hospitals to bring smiles to the faces of young patients, spreading the joy of Christmas to those who can't be at home.

Many hospitals organize special events during the holidays, where children can meet Santa Claus and receive gifts from volunteers.

Fun Fact: In 1979, a group of Los Angeles police officers decided to brighten the spirits of children spending the holidays in the hospital. They donned Santa suits, gathered gifts, and set out to deliver cheer. This act of kindness sparked the 'Santa Cop' tradition, which has since spread across the United States and beyond. Today, police officers, firefighters, and volunteers dressed as Santa, elves, and other beloved characters continue to visit hospitals, bringing joy and laughter to young patients.

How to Get Involved: Contact local hospitals or healthcare centers to inquire about volunteer opportunities during the Christmas season.

adopting families 🍀

Some organizations facilitate "Adopt-a-Family" programs, where generous individuals or groups provide gifts, food, and necessities to families facing financial difficulties.

Adopt-a-Family programs were initially established to help families in crisis during the holiday season, ensuring they have a memorable Christmas.

Fun Fact: Some 'Adopt-a-Family' programs not only provide gifts and essentials but also organize special events or experiences for the families they support. This might include arranging holiday-themed outings, inviting families to participate in festive activities, or even hosting surprise visits from Santa Claus, creating cherished memories that go beyond material gifts.

How to Get Involved: Participate in a local Adopt-a-Family initiative by providing gifts, necessities, or holiday meals for families in need.

christmas charity concerts 🎸

Musicians, choirs, and performers often organize benefit concerts during the holiday season to raise funds for causes like medical research, homelessness, and disaster relief.

Christmas charity concerts often feature popular artists and performers who donate their talents to raise funds for various causes.

Fun Fact: In 1984, the charity supergroup Band Aid released the iconic holiday single 'Do They Know It's Christmas?' Written by Bob Geldof and Midge Ure, this song aimed to raise funds for famine relief in Ethiopia. It featured some of the biggest British and Irish music stars of the time, including Bono, George Michael, and Sting. The song became a massive success and not only raised millions for its cause but also inspired similar charitable efforts worldwide, including the USA for Africa's 'We Are the World' and the 1985 'Live Aid' concert.

How to Get Involved: Attend charity concerts or consider organizing a fundraising event to support a cause close to your heart.

toy drives for shelter pets 🐶 🐱

Animal shelters also receive extra love during Christmas, as people donate toys, food, and supplies to make the holidays special for furry friends awaiting adoption.

During the holiday season, animal shelters advocate for responsible pet adoption, echoing the 'Dog for Life' campaign's message: 'A dog is for life, not just for Christmas®.'

Fun Fact: Some animal shelters have reported receiving donations for more unusual guests, such as rabbits, guinea pigs, and even the occasional parrot.

How to Get Involved: Donate pet food, toys, and supplies to local animal shelters. Consider adopting or fostering a pet in need.

christmas card campaigns

Sending cards to troops, seniors, or individuals in care facilities brightens their holiday season and lets them know they're remembered.

Many organizations facilitate card-writing campaigns to send holiday greetings to troops, seniors, and individuals in care facilities.

Fun Fact: During World War II, to help troops stay connected with their loved ones, a special letter system called 'V-Mail' or 'Victory Mail' was introduced. These letters were designed to be compact and efficiently transported overseas. Instead of sending physical letters, these 'V-Mail' messages were photographed onto microfilm, which saved valuable cargo space on planes and ships. Once developed, the microfilmed letters were printed and delivered to soldiers, allowing them to receive heartfelt messages from home despite the distance.

How to Get Involved: Participate in card-making events, write heartfelt messages, and contribute to sending love and warmth to those who may feel isolated during the holidays.

giving tuesday 🤍

While not directly on Christmas Day, Giving Tuesday falls on the Tuesday following Thanksgiving and serves as a modern tradition of giving back during the holiday season. It's a global movement encouraging people to donate to charitable causes, volunteer their time, or engage in acts of kindness.

Giving Tuesday was first observed in 2012 and has gained momentum over the years as a counterbalance to the consumerism associated with Black Friday and Cyber Monday.

Fun Fact: One of the most heartwarming Giving Tuesday initiatives took place in 2020 when a retired engineer named Terry Wallis decided to give back in a unique way. In what he called the "Trees for Dollars" campaign, he pledged to plant a tree for every dollar donated to the Arbor Day Foundation on that day. What started as a personal project quickly gained traction, and with the support of generous donors, over 150,000 trees were planted across the United States.

How to Get Involved: Donate to reputable nonprofits, volunteer some time at a local charity, food bank, animal shelter or community center. Shop from local businesses, artisans and makers. Or shop with businesses who donate a portion of their proceeds to charity on Giving Tuesday.

a special note from the author

Additional information and links for how you can get involved with these and other charities can be found on the resource section on my website:

knowledgenuggetbooks.com/resources

20
quotable christmas quotes

In the enchanting world of Christmas, words **have the power** to capture the essence of the season's magic and warmth. In this chapter, discover a selection of memorable quoteable Christmas quotes, each offering a glimpse into the heart of this cherished holiday. These words remind us that Christmas is not just a day on the calendar; it's a state of mind filled with love, generosity, and the joy of giving.

"Christmas waves a magic wand over this world, and behold, everything is softer and more beautiful." - Norman Vincent Peale

"Christmas is not a time nor a season, but a state of mind. To cherish peace and goodwill, to be plenteous in mercy, is to have the real spirit of Christmas." - Calvin Coolidge

"Gifts of time and love are surely the basic
ingredients of a truly merry Christmas." -
Peg Bracken

"Christmas will always be as long as we stand
heart to heart and hand in hand." - Dr.
Seuss

"Christmas is the day that holds all of time
together." - Alexander Smith

"The joy of brightening other lives, bearing each
others' burdens, easing other's loads and
supplanting empty hearts and lives with
generous gifts becomes for us the magic of
Christmas." - W.C. Jones

"Christmas is the spirit of giving without a
thought of getting. It is happiness because
we see joy in people. It is forgetting self and
finding time for others." - Thomas S.
Monson

"Our hearts grow tender with childhood memories and love of kindred, and we are better
throughout the year for having, in spirit,
become a child again at Christmastime." -
Laura Ingalls Wilder

"Christmas is a season not only of rejoicing but
of reflection." - Winston Churchill

quotable christmas movie quotes 💬

"It's not what's under the Christmas tree that matters, it's who's around it." - A Charlie Brown Christmas

"The best way to spread Christmas cheer is singing loud for all to hear." - Buddy the Elf, from the movie 'Elf'

"Every time a bell rings, an angel gets his wings." - It's a Wonderful Life

"Just remember, the true spirit of Christmas lies in your heart." - The Polar Express

"Seeing is believing, but sometimes the most real things in the world are the things we can't see." - The Polar Express

"Merry Christmas, ya filthy animal!" - Home Alone 2: Lost in New York

"Nobody's walking out on this fun, old-fashioned family Christmas!" - National Lampoon's Christmas Vacation

"Maybe Christmas, he thought, doesn't come from a store. Maybe Christmas... perhaps... means a little bit more." - How the Grinch Stole Christmas

"If you look for it, I've got a sneaky feeling you'll find that love actually is all around." - Love Actually

"Just because I cannot see it, doesn't mean I can't believe it!" - The Nightmare Before Christmas

21
christmas quiz

'Twas the quiz before Christmas, and all through the book, Twenty questions await, so come take a look. From traditions to stories, and facts old and new, Test your yuletide knowledge; there's much to pursue. So grab your hot cocoa and gather 'round here, Let's dive into Christmas with holiday cheer.

1. Which country has a Christmas tradition involving "Yule Lads," a group of mischievous troll-like characters?

    1. Iceland
    2. Norway
    3. Finland
    4. Denmark

2. In which country is "KFC" (Kentucky Fried Chicken) a popular Christmas Eve meal?

1. USA
2. Canada
3. Japan
4. China

3. Which country is known for the tradition of hiding a pickle ornament in the Christmas tree?

1. Canada
2. Australia
3. Austria
4. Germany

4. In which country would Santa most likely find a mince pie and sherry left out for him?

1. Germany
2. United Kingdom
3. Australia
4. USA

5. Stollen, a fruit bread filled with nuts, spices, and candied fruit, and dusted with powdered sugar, would most likely be found on tables in which country around Christmastime?

1. Spain
2. Italy
3. Brazil
4. Germany

6. All Christians celebrate Christmas on December 25:

   1. True
   2. False

7. In Australia, where Christmas falls during summer, Santa might be depicted wearing a red suit with shorts and sunglasses, reflecting the warm climate.

   1. True
   2. False

8. Dressing up like Father Christmas was once banned in England.

   1. True
   2. False

9. In the Christmas song, "We Wish You a Merry Christmas" what is meant by "figgy pudding?"

   1. Chocolate pudding
   2. Mince pie
   3. Christmas tamale
   4. Christmas pudding

10. The tradition of decorating Christmas trees with spider webs made from silver or gold thread comes from where?

   1. Ukraine
   2. Iceland
   3. Denmark
   4. France

11. The tradition of NORAD tracking Santa started in 1955 when a Sears advertisement misprinted a telephone number for children to call Santa. The number actually connected to the Continental Air Defense Command (CONAD), NORAD's predecessor.

1. True
2. False

12. From which famous Christmas story does the iconic phrase "Bah, humbug!" come from?

1. The Polar Express
2. The Night Before Christmas
3. A Christmas Carol
4. How the Grinch Stole Christmas

13. Which of these Christmas songs was the first to be broadcast from space in a Christmas-themed prank by Gemini 6 astronauts in 1965.

1. Jingle Bells
2. White Christmas
3. We Wish You a Merry Christmas
4. Here Comes Santa Claus

14. "Deck the Halls" was originally a Welsh New Year's Eve carol before it became associated with Christmas

1. True
2. False

15. The first tree ornaments were apples, used to represent the Tree of Knowledge from the Christian tradition.

 1. True
 2. False

16. December has the highest number of wedding proposals and birthdays.

 1. True
 2. False

17. In England, instead of Ugly Christmas sweaters, they wear Ugly Christmas rash guards.

 1. True
 2. False

18. According to a survey by the Greeting Card Association, what is the most popular Christmas card color?

 1. Gold
 2. Silver
 3. Green
 4. Red

19. Which of the following is NOT one of Santa's reindeer?

 1. Dancer
 2. Blitzen
 3. Sparkle
 4. Comet

20. Match the name of Santa Claus and the country it's used in:

1. Father Christmas
2. Père Noël
3. Babbo Natale
4. Sinterklaas
5. Weihnachtsmann
6. San Nicolás
7. Joulupukki
8. Hoteiosho

Finland: ____
Japan: ____
United Kingdom: ____
France: ____
Italy: ____
Germany: ____
Netherlands: ____
Venezuela: ____

22
christmas quiz answers

Twas the moment you waited for, no more mystery to keep, After pondering questions, it's time for a peep. We've unwrapped the solutions, like gifts on display, To illuminate your path in a festive array. So sit back and enjoy, as the responses unfold, The magic of Christmas, in stories retold.

1. Which country has a Christmas tradition involving "Yule Lads," a group of mischievous troll-like characters?

  1. **Iceland**
  2. Norway
  3. Finland
  4. Denmark

2. In which country is "KFC" (Kentucky Fried Chicken) a popular Christmas Eve meal?

1. USA
2. Canada
3. **Japan**
4. China

3. Which country is known for the tradition of hiding a pickle ornament in the Christmas tree?

1. Canada
2. Australia
3. Austria
4. **Germany**

4. In which country would Santa most likely find a mince pie and sherry left out for him?

1. Germany
2. **United Kingdom**
3. Australia
4. USA

5. Stollen, a fruit bread filled with nuts, spices, and candied fruit, and dusted with powdered sugar, would most likely be found on tables in which country around Christmastime?

1. Spain
2. Italy
3. Brazil
4. **Germany**

6. All Christians celebrate Christmas on December 25.

   1. True
   2. **False**

7. In Australia, where Christmas falls during summer, Santa might be depicted wearing a red suit with shorts and sunglasses, reflecting the warm climate.

   1. **True**
   2. False

8. Dressing up like Father Christmas was once banned in England.

   1. True
   2. **False**

9. In the Christmas song, "We Wish You a Merry Christmas" what is meant by "figgy pudding?"

   1. Chocolate pudding
   2. Mince pie
   3. Christmas tamale
   4. **Christmas pudding**

10. The tradition of decorating Christmas trees with spider webs made from silver or gold thread comes from which country?

   1. **Ukraine**
   2. Iceland

3. Denmark
4. France

11. The tradition of NORAD tracking Santa started in 1955 when a Sears advertisement misprinted a telephone number for children to call Santa. The number actually connected to the Continental Air Defense Command (CONAD), NORAD's predecessor.

1. **True**
2. False

12. From which famous Christmas story does the iconic phrase "Bah, humbug!" come from?

1. The Polar Express
2. The Night Before Christmas
3. **A Christmas Carol**
4. How the Grinch Stole Christmas

13. Which of these Christmas songs was the first to be broadcast from space in a Christmas-themed prank by Gemini 6 astronauts in 1965.

1. **Jingle Bells**
2. White Christmas
3. We Wish You a Merry Christmas
4. Here Comes Santa Claus

14. "Deck the Halls" was originally a Welsh New Year's Eve carol before it became associated with Christmas

  1. **<u>True</u>**
  2. False

15. The first tree ornaments were apples, used to represent the Tree of Knowledge from the Christian tradition.

  1. **<u>True</u>**
  2. False

16. December has the highest number of wedding proposals and birthdays.

  1. True
  2. **<u>False</u>**

17. In England, instead of Ugly Christmas sweaters, they wear Ugly Christmas rash guards.

  1. True
  2. **<u>False</u>**

18. According to a survey by the Greeting Card Association, what is the most popular Christmas card color?

  1. Gold
  2. Silver
  3. Green
  4. **<u>Red</u>**

19. Which of the following is NOT one of Santa's reindeer?

1. Dancer
2. Blitzen
3. **Sparkle**
4. Comet

20. Match the name of Santa Claus and the country it's used in:

Finland: 7. Joulupukki
Japan: 8. Hoteiosho
United Kingdom: 1. Father Christmas
France: 2. Père Noël
Italy: 3. Babbo Natale
Germany: 5. Weihnachtsmann
Netherlands: 4. Sinterklaas
Venezuela: 6. San Nicolás

have a christmas tradition or fun fact you think i missed?

I couldn't fit everything into this first book, so I'm sure I missed some good ones. I'm always on the hunt for the weird, the wonderful, and the downright bizarre when it comes to Christmas Traditions around the World! If you know of a fun and unique Christmas or holiday tradition that you think deserves a spotlight, I'd love to hear about it.

Your suggestion could even make it into a future edition of "Christmas Fun Facts!"

How to Submit:

Describe the Tradition: Tell me what the tradition or fun fact entails, where it's located, and why it's you think it should be included.

Include Anecdotes: Got a fun story or surprising fact about the tradition? I'd love to hear it!

Provide References: If possible, include articles, websites, or contacts where I can learn more.

Submission Instructions:

• Email your submissions to hello@ knowledgenuggetbooks.com

• Use the subject line: "Christmas Tradition Submission: [Name of the Tradition]"

Selected entries may be featured in future editions, newsletters, or even become the topic of my next deep-dive blog article!

I can't wait to hear what you have to share! Thank you!

caught the christmas cheer?

If this book filled your stocking with joy and newfound Christmas tidbits, I'd be twinkling like a star on top of the tree to hear your thoughts in a heartwarming review.

Your merry feedback is the gift that keeps on giving, and it'd be a Christmas miracle to hear from you!

Jingle all the way
to where you unwrapped this book and leave your festive review: bit.ly/christmas-factbook-review

Is Goodreads your winter wonderland?
Spread the Christmas cheer there too: www.goodreads.com

Sending snowy thank-yous and holiday hugs your way!

acknowledgments

Writing a book is like decorating a Christmas tree—it's a team effort that makes it truly sparkle. As we delve into the Christmas traditions and holiday curiosities, I want to give a warm shoutout to the remarkable individuals who've made this journey merry and bright.

It's with immense gratitude that I extend my heartfelt thanks to each and every one of you, as your contributions have truly transformed this book into a festive and joyful celebration of the holiday season.

To William Harang, Loretta Crow, and Janet Hale-Sanders, my invaluable beta readers, your insightful feedback, brilliant suggestions and unwavering support were essential in shaping this book into what it is today.

My heartfelt thanks go to my editor, Joe Levit, whose expertise and dedication elevated the quality of this project. Special recognition is due to my meticulous fact checker, Hank Musolf, for ensuring the accuracy of every fun fact shared within these pages.

A big shout-out to the incredibly talented book designer, Paul Hawkins, whose creative touch not only graces the cover but also adds a festive and magical flair to the interior. Your contributions have truly made this book shine.

Special thanks to ChatGPT by OpenAI for being an ever-reliable brainstorming partner and virtual writing assistant. Whether it was generating ideas or fine-tuning the text, this cutting-edge technology played a role in making this book what it is. Together, we've brought these Christmas fun facts to life, and I'm incredibly grateful for the collaboration.

To my amazing wife, your unwavering support, encouragement, and contributions to this Christmas fun fact book have been nothing short of remarkable. From being an additional editor, brilliant proofreader, and chief cheerleader to lending a hand with festive research and fact-checking, you've played an essential role in bringing this holiday collection to life. Your dedication and love have transformed this project into a joyful journey, and I couldn't have done it without you. You're not just my life partner; you're my muse, my collaborator, and my favorite co-author. Thank you for being the shining star on top of this literary Christmas tree!

To all those who played a part in making this Christmas fun fact book a reality, whether through encouragement, guidance, or direct involvement, your support has been the greatest gift of all. May these festive pages bring joy, knowledge, and a touch of holiday magic to your lives. Merry Christmas and Happy Holidays to each and every one of you!

don't forget your jolly gift!

Ho, ho, ho! As a token of appreciation for joining our festive journey, I've whipped up a FREE companion quiz e-book, brimming with over 100 jolly questions and answers straight from these pages.

Get your FREE festive quiz e-book right here:
🔗 https://bit.ly/christmas-factbook-bonus

SCAN ME

Challenge your friends, and spread the joy!
Merry Quizzing and Happy Holidays!

meet the author behind
the tinsel

Marianne Jennings, with a twinkle in her eye reminiscent of the North Star, ventures through life with the joyous spirit of a child on Christmas morning. Esteemed by her ten nieces and nephews as the best storyteller (and cookie baker) this side of the North Pole, she fills their lives with tales, laughter, and the magic of Christmas.

Her fascination for Yuletide trivia? It's as profound as an elf's love for candy canes and gift-wrapping marathons. With a heart full of festive warmth and a sleigh-load of fun facts, Marianne's aim is to gift the world snippets of joy, wrapped in tidbits of fascinating truths.

For a dash more Christmas cheer, a sleigh ride of facts, or a hearty holiday chat, meet Marianne under the mistletoe at https://knowledgenuggetbooks.com or jingle alongside her festive posts on Instagram.

also by marianne jennings

So You Think You Know Canada, Eh?

This collection of silly & interesting facts is about Canada, the kind people who live there, all things maple syrup, hockey & lacrosse, its unique history, the breathtaking nature, & words to help you speak Canadian.

Amazing Alaska!

From glaciers to grizzlies, this #1 Bestseller in Alaska Travel is sure to surprise and delight readers who love anything and everything about Alaska. Packed with over 700 fun and interesting fun facts that even most locals don't know.

Everything About Astronauts Vol. 1 & Vol. 2

Teens and adults who love astronauts, fun facts, and little-known stories will find themselves mesmerized with over 1,400 interesting facts and out-of-world stories.

Quirky Careers & Offbeat Occupations

of the Past, Present, and Future

Explore a world where careers go beyond the ordinary 9 to 5. Whether you're intrigued by history, curious about niche careers, or dream of futuristic roles this collection of over 240 unique careers will entertain, educate, and inspire.

Printed in Great Britain
by Amazon

34935166R00119